Marriage COVENANT

THE BIBLICAL SECRET FOR A
LOVE THAT LASTS

DEREK PRINCE

WHITAKER
HOUSE

MARRIAGE COVENANT:
The Biblical Secret for a Love That Lasts
Revised and Expanded Edition

Derek Prince Ministries
P.O. Box 19501
Charlotte, NC 28219-9501
www.derekprince.org

ISBN: 978-0-88368-781-9
eBook ISBN: 978-1-60374-442-3
Printed in the United States of America
© 1978, 2006 by Derek Prince Ministries, International

Whitaker House
1030 Hunt Valley Circle
New Kensington, PA 15068
www.whitakerhouse.com

```
┌─────────────────────────────────────────────────────────┐
│      Library of Congress Cataloging-in-Publication Data   │
│  Prince, Derek.                                           │
│    Marriage covenant : the biblical secret for a love     │
│  that lasts / by Derek Prince. —Rev. and expanded ed.     │
│      p.   cm.                                             │
│    ISBN-13: 978-0-88368-781-9 (trade pbk.)                │
│    ISBN-10: 0-88368-781-X (trade pbk.)                    │
│    1. Marriage—Religious aspects—Christianity. 2. Marriage│
│  —Biblical teaching. I. Title.                            │
│    BV835.P77 2006                                         │
│    248.8'44—dc22                                          │
│                            2006008975                     │
└─────────────────────────────────────────────────────────┘
```

15 16 **UI** 25 24

Contents

Foreword

BY RUTH PRINCE

S oon after I came to know the Lord Jesus as my Savior and Messiah in 1970, I came into contact with real Christians whose marriages were a constant testimony to His lordship in their lives. At about the same time, I became acquainted with the teaching and ministry of Derek Prince, Charles Simpson, and others. As a single woman, my prayer to God was, "Set me under authority, in the place You have for me, that I may serve You in the best way and help to prepare for the coming of Your kingdom."

My prayers were answered several years later, in a way that I had not anticipated, when God chose me to be Derek's wife, his new *"help meet"* (Genesis 2:18 KJV). Derek's first wife, Lydia, was an extraordinary woman who laid down her life and her own successful ministry in Jerusalem for her husband. When Derek married her in 1946, she was a respected spiritual leader there with an established work of her own.[1] However, she accepted willingly the behind-the-scenes role of intercessor, homemaker, supporter—that of a true wife.

When I first came into close personal contact with Derek, I was impressed by the way he lived out his teaching in his personal conduct; he "practiced what he preached." I have come to see that much of his present ability to minister to the needs of God's people has its roots in the relationship he and Lydia had with one another for almost thirty years and in their relationship, as a unit, with the Lord.

Most of the material contained in *Marriage Covenant* was developed and taught before I came into Derek's life. Yet, in the same period of time, while I was living in Jerusalem completely out of touch with his ministry and teaching, the Holy Spirit was speaking to me along the same lines about the real meaning of covenant. My study led me to Genesis chapter 15. I identified with the experience of Abraham as he entered into a deep, personal, life-changing relationship

---

[1] Lydia's own dramatic story is told by Derek in their book, *Appointment in Jerusalem,* published just before her death in 1975. The 30th anniversary edition is available from Whitaker House.

with God—a relationship so profound that we still refer to our God as "the God of Abraham." It was a life of total commitment.

During the same period, I was also reflecting on the role of women in the body of Christ. I saw that God had created Eve for the sole purpose of meeting Adam's need, that man was not complete without his God-given mate. It seems to me that in contemporary Western society, and in much of the church, too many women are endeavoring (often loudly) to do something they were never created to do—to succeed in life as independent, solitary entities. For a number of years, I myself sought fulfillment in that way as a career woman. But when I entered into a relationship with Jesus, my life was redirected. I began to see that it is women who are the losers when they neglect the marriage covenant—along with the men who are not able to achieve the wholeness God intended for them in union with their mates.

I realize that it is not possible for every man and every woman to find that ideal mate and that it certainly is better to be alone with the Lord than to be unequally yoked with an unbeliever. For many, there is no other choice than to remain single. The quality of the single life, with which I am well acquainted, can be determined by the quality of the relationship with God and the relationship with other Christians. Commitment seems to be the key—commitment to God, to His will for your life, and to that part of the body of Christ with which you are connected.

It seems appropriate that the first publishing of this book is just as Derek and I are joining our lives in the covenant of marriage. At the same time, I am joining myself to the part of the body with which he is associated in the United States, and he with the part of the body to which I belong in Jerusalem. We believe we are conforming to God's preordained plan as we each lay down our life for the other, that we may merge into one new entity under the lordship of Jesus. We know that, as with everything in the spiritual life, this must be walked out on a day-to-day basis. I believe that this book contains not only the pattern, but also the practical instruction on how to do so.

I pray that applying the principles of this book will lead you, whether you are a man or a woman, into the wholeness that God wills for you, in covenant relationship with Himself and with His people.

—*Ruth Prince*
1978

ONE

Marriage Is a Covenant

CHAPTER 1

Marriage Is a Covenant

Is there a secret to a successful marriage? Why do some couples succeed and others fail? Is it all just a matter of chance?

One thing is certain: If there is a secret that ensures a successful marriage, millions of couples in our contemporary culture have never found it. In almost every country in Western civilization, the proportion of divorces to marriages has soared dramatically in the last few decades. In the United States, we have reached a situation where there is approximately one divorce for every two marriages. Fifty years ago, a person familiar with American life would never have dreamed that such a situation could arise in so short a period.

However, the ratio of divorces to marriages does not tell the whole story. Many marriages that have not yet ended in the final shipwreck of divorce nevertheless find themselves in very troubled and unhappy circumstances. In some cases, there is open strife and disharmony, usually involving all those who live under the one roof, both parents and children. In other cases, although things appear fairly calm on the surface, underneath there are the festering sores of bitterness, unforgiveness, and rebellion. Sooner or later, these are liable to erupt in the form of some mental or emotional breakdown, the cause of which may never be precisely diagnosed.

Those who are specifically concerned with mental health have suggested that about one out of every four persons in America today either needs, or will need, some form of psychiatric care. Psychiatric treatment centers are overflowing, and professional psychiatrists are in ever increasing demand. This has a direct bearing on the condition of marriage and the home, because it is generally agreed that the majority of mental and emotional problems can be traced back to tension and disharmony in the home, primarily in marriage relationships. Thus, the progressive deterioration of mental and emotional health is one of many symptoms in contemporary society that point to the most urgent social problem of our day—the break-down of marriage and the home.

The reaction of certain contemporary sociologists to this situation has taken the form of passively accepting the inevitable. Some have even gone so far as to assert that the concept of marriage was a "mistake" in the first place and that it is no longer relevant in our present "advanced" state of social progress. However, many of the so-called experts who make such pronouncements are themselves the product of

> THERE IS A SECRET
> THAT CAN ENSURE
> A SUCCESSFUL
> MARRIAGE.

unhappy homes; more than a few also have the record of at least one unsuccessful marriage in their own lives. We may therefore have grounds to inquire whether their statements to the effect that marriage is irrelevant or outmoded do not merely put them on the level of the fox in Aesop's fable. He had tried desperately to reach a cluster of luscious grapes, but failed. His final comment was, "They're probably sour anyway!"

In the face of this confused situation and these conflicting opinions, I want to state, clearly and briefly, my own personal conviction. I believe that there is a secret that can ensure a successful marriage. Furthermore, I believe that this secret is revealed in the pages of one unique book—the Bible.

Before I proceed to explain what this secret is, it will be appropriate for me to give a little of my own personal background. This could be interpreted as presenting my credentials and qualifications for addressing this subject.

Personal Background

I was educated at two of Britain's most famous educational institutions—Eton College and Cambridge University. Prior to World War II, I pursued a career in philosophy, and in 1940 I was elected to a fellowship (resident professorship) in this field at King's College, Cambridge. However, the impact of World War II interrupted my academic career.

In 1941, while serving as a hospital attendant in the British army, I had a dramatic, life-changing encounter with God—something that was totally out of line with my previous philosophic theories and preconceptions. Out of this encounter, I formed two conclusions that I have never since had reason to change: first, that Jesus Christ is alive; second, that the Bible is a true, relevant, up-to-date book. These two conclusions radically and permanently altered the whole course of my life.

When I was in Jerusalem in 1946, I married a Danish lady, Lydia Christensen, who was the "mother" of a small home for girls that she had founded there. Through my marriage to Lydia, in one day I became the adoptive father of eight girls, of whom six were Jewish, one was Arab, and one was English. Also at this time, I studied for two years at the Hebrew University in Jerusalem. Lydia and I and our eight girls continued living in Jerusalem throughout the upheavals that marked the birth of the State of Israel. We thus came face to face, as a family, with the grim realities of siege, famine, and war. Later we moved, still as a family, to Britain.

In the years that followed, I served in various capacities in various lands: as a pastor in Britain; as an educator in Kenya; as a Bible teacher and conference speaker in Europe, Canada, the United States, New Zealand, Australia, and other countries. Throughout all my travels, Lydia was always by my side. Sometimes, after we had been ministering together in public, people would make the comment,

"The two of you work together as if you were one person."

In Kenya, Lydia and I adopted our ninth child, an African baby girl. We successfully completed the raising of all our nine girls. At the time of this writing, all but our youngest have married and have presented us with many grandchildren.[2]

After thirty years, my marriage with Lydia was terminated by her death. Our life together had always been an open book—not only to our children, but also to countless people who, through the years, came to our home for counseling and prayer.

> "THE TWO OF YOU WORK TOGETHER AS IF YOU WERE ONE PERSON."

Of all those who knew us in this way, I question whether there are any who would not agree that our marriage was happy and successful. Certainly it had its fair share of tensions and problems—more than would be experienced by a "normal" couple who spend their whole life in one familiar setting. But the success of a

---

[2] Note: All of Derek Prince's daughters have since married.

marriage does not depend upon the absence of tensions and problems; it depends upon a special quality of relationship that needs to be developed between husband and wife.

In the pages that follow, it is my intention to share with you the secret of how to build a relationship of this kind. I trust that the brief outline of my life to this point will be sufficient to demonstrate that my convictions are not just a set of abstract theories that have never been put to the tests of real life.

Perhaps I should add that at the moment of writing I am about to remarry. Coincidentally, I met my second wife, Ruth, like my first, in Jerusalem. I enter this second marriage with a quiet trust that God will also crown this marriage with His blessing, as Ruth and I meet the conditions that He has revealed in Scripture.[3]

Marriage Is a Mystery

In Ephesians 5:22–32, Paul explained the Christian view of marriage. He concluded by saying, *"This mystery is great"* (v. 32). Thus, he acknowledged that marriage is a mystery. In Paul's time, the word *mystery* had a more

---

[3] Note: Derek and Ruth remained happily married until her death in 1998. Together, they traveled and ministered around the world, fulfilling the Great Commission.

specific meaning than it does today. Then, it had religious associations. It denoted a form of knowledge that conferred valuable benefits but was restricted to a special group who were bound together by their religious practices. For a person to have access to this knowledge, he first had to be initiated into the group.

Thus, Paul's use of the word *mystery* to describe the marriage relationship suggests two things: first, that there is a little-known form of knowledge that can make marriage what it ought to be; second, that a person can acquire this knowledge only by undergoing certain tests and meeting certain conditions. It is the main purpose of this book to initiate the reader into these tests and conditions.

In the book of Deuteronomy, when the children of Israel were ready to enter into their promised inheritance in the land of Canaan, Moses reviewed for them the kind of lifestyle God had planned for them in their new environment. He promised them, on God's behalf, that if they would keep God's law, they would be abundantly blessed in every area of their lives. In particular, Moses told them that their homes would be like *"heaven upon...earth"* (Deuteronomy 11:21 KJV). He painted a beautiful picture of contentment and unbroken harmony. Such was the level of home life God had planned for His people.

About twelve hundred years later, through the prophet Malachi, God took stock of Israel's conduct since they had entered into their inheritance. In general, they had failed to meet God's conditions and therefore had not enjoyed the level of life He had planned for them. In His assessment, God pinpointed a number of specific areas of failure. One was in the Israelites' home lives, and specifically in their marriages. Here is what the Lord said concerning this:

> *And this is another thing you do: you cover the altar of the Lord with tears, with weeping and with groaning, because He no longer regards the offering or accepts it with favor from your hand. Yet you say, "For what reason?" Because the Lord has been a witness between you and the wife of your youth, against whom you have dealt treacherously, though she is your companion and your wife by covenant.* (Malachi 2:13–14)

Obviously, Israel's failure in this respect was not due to lack of religion. They were *"cover*[ing] *the altar of the* LORD *with tears."* Yet, for all their prayers, their marriages were failures. We are quite often confronted with a similar situation today. People may be very busy with religious activities and yet be unable to make a success of their marriages. Their religion does not enable them to succeed at home. Indeed, excessive preoccupation with religion outside the home, by one or both parties, is sometimes an important factor in the failure of a marriage.

> WHEN MARRIAGE LOSES ITS SANCTITY, IT ALSO LOSES ITS STRENGTH AND STABILITY.

The essence of Israel's failure is contained in the closing phrase of Malachi 2:14: *"though she is...your wife by covenant."* Israel had come to view marriage as a relationship for which they might set their own standards, one that they were free to initiate or terminate on their own terms. God reminded them, however, that He views marriage quite differently. According to His unchanging purpose, marriage is a covenant, which is the secret that alone ensures the success of the marriage relationship.

Once this secret is forgotten or ignored, marriage inevitably loses its sanctity. When marriage loses its sanctity, it also loses its strength and stability. Much of what we see in our contemporary civilization is closely parallel to the condition of Israel in Malachi's day, and the root cause is the same—a wrong view of marriage.

Jesus' Standard of Marriage

After Malachi, the next and fuller revelation of marriage comes to us through Jesus. The essence of His teaching on marriage is contained in a conversation He had with some Pharisees:

And some Pharisees came to Him, testing Him, and saying, "Is it lawful for a man to divorce his wife for any cause at all?" And He answered and said, "Have you not read, that He who created them from the beginning made them male and female, and said, 'For this cause a man shall leave his father and mother, and shall cleave to his wife; and the two shall become one flesh'? Consequently they are no more two, but one flesh. What therefore God has joined together, let no man separate." They said to Him, "Why then did Moses command to give her a certificate of divorce and send her away?" He said to them, "Because of your hardness of heart, Moses permitted you to divorce your wives; but from the beginning it has not been this way. And I say to you, whoever divorces his wife, except for immorality, and marries another woman commits adultery."   (Matthew 19:3–9)

In the movie *Fiddler on the Roof*, the rabbi in the village is depicted periodically teaching his young students about Jewish Law and spiritual things. At one point in the movie, he says that, among other things, if a wife burns the cake she is baking, that's grounds for divorce. There are many rabbinical laws that deal explicitly with how and when divorce is supposedly acceptable.

JESUS ALWAYS WENT BACK TO GOD'S ORIGINAL INTENTION FOR MARRIAGE.

When Jesus taught about marriage, however, He never accepted the current Jewish standard. He always went back to God's original intention for marriage. Here, His remarks were prefaced by *"from the beginning."* In Hebrew, the book of Genesis is called *In the Beginning.* So, when Jesus said those words, He was directing His questioners back to the Genesis record of creation, which is the basis of all His teaching on marriage and the first record we have of the joining of man and wife. He didn't accept the standards prevalent in the Judaism of the day; He always went back to His Father's original plan, unfolded in the garden of Eden.

We may sum up the teaching of Jesus in this passage in four successive statements:

1. The form of marriage that had become accepted in Israel under Judaism was below the level of God's will.

2. God's real purpose for marriage was expressed when He originally created man and woman.

3. In the initial union of man and woman, they were so perfectly joined together that they lost their separate identities and became "one flesh."

4. It is the purpose of Jesus to restore marriage in the lives of His disciples to the original standard revealed at creation.

If we consider the account in the first and second chapters of Genesis of the creation and union of Adam and Eve, one fact is emphasized throughout: God Himself was directly and personally involved. It was His decision, not Adam's, that Adam should have a mate; it was He who formed Eve from Adam; it was He who presented her to Adam; and it was He who established the terms of the covenant relationship in which He united them.

Therefore, it is correct to say that, all through the Old Testament, marriage was viewed as a covenant relationship. However, the concept that developed under Judaism was on a lower level than that which had found expression at creation. Under Judaism, the covenant relationship was viewed as being merely horizontal—between a man and a woman. But the covenant relationship established at creation had two dimensions— horizontal and vertical. Horizontally, it related Adam and Eve to each other; but vertically, it related the two of them together to God.

THE COVENANT RELATIONSHIP ESTABLISHED AT CREATION HAD TWO DIMENSIONS— HORIZONTAL AND VERTICAL.

"A Cord of Three Strands"

A passage in Ecclesiastes expresses in allegorical terms the difference between these two levels of marriage:

> *Two are better than one because they have a good return for their labor. For if either of them falls, the one will lift up his companion. But woe to the one who falls when there is not another to lift him up. Furthermore, if two lie down together they keep warm, but how can one be warm alone? And if one can overpower him who is alone, two can resist him. A cord of three strands is not quickly torn apart.* (Ecclesiastes 4:9–12)

The principle from which Solomon started, *"Two are better than one,"* agrees with the reason that God gave originally for providing a mate for Adam: *"It is not good for the man to be alone"* (Genesis 2:18). Solomon went on to give three examples that clearly illustrate this principle: when two are together and one falls, the other can help him up; if two lie down together, they keep each other warm; if two are attacked, together they can drive off the attacker. But the last example that Solomon gives is different: "A *cord of three strands is not quickly torn apart."* In this case, the strength is supplied not merely by two together, but by three together.

We may use Solomon's pictures to illustrate the difference we have observed between the concept of marriage under Judaism and the concept of marriage that was initiated by God Himself at creation. Solomon's first three examples of "two together" illustrate the concept of marriage on the human plane, a horizontal relationship, merely between a man and a woman. But Solomon's fourth picture—the *"cord of three strands"*—illustrates marriage as it was conceived at creation, a binding together of three persons: a man, a woman, and God. The relationship between the man and the woman is still on the human plane; but when God is added to the relationship, it introduces a new dimension. He becomes an integral part of the marriage.

One of the most revolutionary features of the teaching of Jesus was His standard of marriage. He refused to settle for anything less than the original purpose of God. For this reason, Solomon's picture of *"a cord of three strands"* not only illustrates the pattern of marriage established at creation, but it also portrays just as accurately the pattern of marriage for believers today who are united through their faith in Christ. The principle that binds them inseparably together is *covenant*. What Solomon said of a cord thus formed is still true today; it *"is not quickly torn apart."*

Some time ago, I was speaking in New Zealand on this picture of Christian marriage as a cord of three strands. At the end of my talk, a man came up and introduced himself. "I am a professional rope maker," he said. "My business is making ropes. I want to tell you that what you

THE PRINCIPLE THAT BINDS BELIEVERS INSEPARABLY TOGETHER IN MARRIAGE IS *COVENANT.*

have said is absolutely true in the practical realm. The strongest rope is a threefold rope."

Then he went on to give me the following explanation: The largest number of strands that can all touch one another is three. If you take away one and leave only two, obviously you weaken the rope. But if you add an extra strand and make four, you do not add to the strength of the rope because all the strands no longer touch one another. If you have a rope of three strands, one—or even two—of the strands may be under pressure and start to fray. But as long as the third strand holds, the rope will not break.

This rope maker's explanation made the picture of Christian marriage as a threefold cord so vivid for me that I went on meditating on it for days. In my mind's eye, I could see the rope under such tremendous strain that two of its strands began to fray. But the third strand remained strong and held out until the strain was eased and the two frayed strands could be bound up.

That's exactly how it is, I thought to myself, *in a truly Christian marriage! There come times of strain when both husband and wife may begin to weaken and feel unable to hold out. But God Himself is that third strand, and He holds on until the strain is eased and both husband and wife can be healed and restored.*

In our comparison of Christian marriage to a cord of three strands, we have said that the principle that intertwines the strands and holds them together is covenant. Clearly, this makes covenant an essential element of a successful marriage. And yet, although covenant is one of the central themes of biblical revelation, most Christians today don't truly understand it.

Therefore, we will now go on in chapter 2 to examine the nature of covenant as it is revealed in Scripture. Then, in chapter 3, we will explain in practical terms just how covenant works to unite a man and a woman in marriage and to hold them together. In chapter 4, we will talk about how you can discover whom God has for you to marry.

In chapters 5 and 6, respectively, we will examine how covenant also serves as the essential binding force in two other vitally important relationships: between God and the individual Christian, and between fellow Christians in their relationship to one another.

Finally, in chapter 7, "The Point of Decision," we will give practical direction to those who feel a need to bring their personal relationship into line with the principles explained in this book.

TWO

The Nature
of Covenant

CHAPTER 2

The Nature of Covenant

What is there in a covenant that gives marriage a strength and stability not otherwise possible? What is the essence of covenant?

The nature of covenant is one of the jealously guarded secrets of Scripture. It is a pearl that God will not cast to the careless. (See Matthew 7:6.) It is something holy that God will not unveil to the impure. In Psalm 25:14, David said, *"The secret of the LORD is for those who fear Him, and He will make them know His covenant."* The secret of covenant, therefore, must be approached in the reverent fear of God. It is withheld from those who approach with any other attitude.

Furthermore, an understanding of covenant requires careful, thorough study of Scripture. It takes time and concentration. In Proverbs 2:4,

Solomon stated that those who desire discernment and understanding must *"seek her as silver, and search for her as for hidden treasures."* This implies strenuous effort. Just as the earth does not yield up her treasures to the superficial observer, so Scripture yields up the true understanding of covenant only to those who are willing to go below the surface and to devote time and study to their search.

I say this by way of introduction to the study of covenant that we will now undertake in this chapter. At first, it may seem somewhat hard and laborious. But if we pursue it with patience and diligence, it will ultimately yield up treasures of infinite worth. These will be the subjects of the succeeding chapters.

The Definition of Covenant

There are two basic words in Scripture for covenant. The Greek word used in the New Testament is *diatheke*. The Hebrew word used in the Old Testament is *b'rit* (or *b'rith*). This Hebrew word occurs in the name of the well-known Jewish organization, *B'nai B'rith*, which means, literally, "Sons of Covenant." Each of these words—*diatheke* in Greek and *b'rit* in Hebrew—is regularly translated by two different English words: *covenant* and *testament*. The English word used in each case varies according to the context.

In English, we do not normally think of *covenant* and *testament* as being the same. We limit the word *testament* to a legal document that, as Scripture points out, comes into force only after the death of the one who made the testament. (See Hebrews 9:16–17 KJV.) On the other hand, we do not usually think of a covenant as being necessarily associated with the death of the parties to the covenant. However, in the concepts of Scripture, this distinction between *testament* and *covenant* is not valid. In Scripture a covenant is a testament, and a testament is a covenant.

> THE CONCEPT OF COVENANT IS CENTRAL TO THE WHOLE OF DIVINE REVELATION.

We are all aware, of course, that the Bible has come to us in the form of two "testaments"—the Old Testament and the New Testament. However, our understanding is increased if we substitute the word *covenant* for *testament* in each case, and speak of the Old

Covenant and the New Covenant. It is a fact of tremendous significance that God's entire written revelation to man is contained in the form of two covenants. Thus, the concept of covenant is central to the whole of divine revelation. If we do not understand the nature of covenant, how far can we hope to understand the real meaning of God's message to us?

What, then, is the meaning of the word *covenant?* It is not easy to give a precise and simple definition. It is suggested that the root meaning of the Hebrew word *b'rit* is "to bind," but that is not certain. It is certain, however, that a covenant is binding. The root meaning of the Greek word *diatheke* is "to set something out in order." It suggests, therefore, the setting forth of specific terms and conditions. It has more of a legal association than its Hebrew counterpart *b'rit.*

In Scripture, we find two different types of covenant. One is on the horizontal plane, a covenant between two human beings. This more nearly approaches the concept of a contract. For instance, in 1 Kings 5:12, we read about Solomon making a covenant with Hiram, the king of Tyre. (The King James Version here translates *b'rit* with the word *"league."*) By this covenant, Solomon and Hiram committed themselves to mutual friendship and established the conditions upon which Hiram would supply Solomon with material and labor for the building of the temple.

Although this form of covenant was only on the human level—between two kings—it is interesting to note that later on, when God declared through the prophet Amos that He would bring judgment on the kingdom of Tyre, one reason that He gave was that they *"did not remember the covenant of brotherhood"* (Amos 1:9)— that is, the covenant made between Solomon and Hiram. So we see that, even on the human level, God considers the breaking of a covenant a very serious matter and one that will bring judgment on the guilty party.

> ESSENTIALLY, A COVENANT EXPRESSES A RELATIONSHIP THAT GOD HIMSELF SOVEREIGNLY INITIATES OUT OF HIS OWN CHOICE AND DECISION.

One should not take entering into a covenant, nor breaking one, lightly.

Covenant, interestingly enough, also is evident in the Hebrew name for the United

States of America. The Hebrew word translates, "lands of the covenant." The fact that the United States was built on a covenant, the Constitution, makes it different from most other nations. We have a "more perfect union" because of the covenant, and we must not turn away from that agreement. Were we to stop abiding by our covenant, our nation would certainly begin to disintegrate.

Covenant: The Basis of Relationship

The main use of covenant in Scripture, however, is not as a contract between two human beings on the horizontal plane, but as a relationship sovereignly initiated by God Himself, with man, in which the two parties are not on the same level. Essentially, a covenant expresses a relationship that God Himself sovereignly initiates out of His own choice and decision. He defines the terms on which He is prepared to enter into that relationship with man.

We need to emphasize that the initiative is wholly with God and the terms are set exclusively by God. Man's part is simply to respond to God's offer of a covenant and to accept the relationship that the covenant brings with it. Man does not set the terms, nor does he ever initiate the relationship. You have to be something of a Calvinist, or at least familiar with the concept of predestination, to grasp and understand this aspect of covenant. Historically, the Calvinist stream of Protestantism has always laid special emphasis on covenant. In so doing, they have preserved a thread of truth that is very important. I would venture to say that we cannot fully understand our relationship with God unless we understand the scriptural concept of covenant.

> GOD NEVER ENTERS INTO A PERMANENT RELATIONSHIP APART FROM A COVENANT.

In the last analysis, every permanent relationship of God with man is based on a covenant. God never enters into a permanent relationship apart from a covenant. In Psalm 50:1–5, the psalmist gave a prophetic preview of the Lord coming in power and glory at the close of this age to gather His people to Himself. In so doing, he clearly defined those whom God will acknowledge as His people.

The Mighty One, God, the Lord, has spoken, and summoned the earth from the rising of the sun to its setting. [This is a call to the whole earth.] *Out of Zion, the perfection of beauty, God has shone forth. May our God come and not keep silence; fire devours before Him, and it is very tempestuous around Him.* [This is a clear prophecy of the coming of the Lord in power, glory, and judgment.] *He summons the heavens above, and the earth, to judge His people:* [This is the judgment of God's people, before the judgment seat of Christ—not the judgment of the unbeliever, but the judgment of the believer. Not the judgment of condemnation, but the judgment for reward.] *"Gather My godly ones to Me, those who have made a covenant with Me by sacrifice."* [This verse tells us to whom God's call is addressed.]   (Psalm 50:1–5)

The Hebrew word here translated *"godly ones"* is *hasid*. It is the word that gives us *hasidic* Judaism—which is the most intense and dedicated form of orthodox Judaism. A *hasid* is a person whose life is totally wrapped up in God. He is a person who exists only for God.

However, the psalmist here defined the *"godly ones,"* the true *hasidim,* as *"those who*

have made a covenant with Me by sacrifice"—
more literally, "those who cut My covenant on
the basis of a sacrifice." The Hebrew speaks
of "cutting" a covenant, rather than merely
making one. It suggests the action of the knife
that puts the sacrifice to death. "My" covenant
means specifically the covenant that God Himself initiated, the eternal covenant. There is only
one basis on which God makes a covenant—the
basis of a sacrifice. Without a sacrifice, there
can be no covenant.

Years ago, about 1944, when I first began
to study the Bible in Hebrew, the Holy Spirit
prompted me to do something unusual. I armed
myself with three colored pencils—blue, green,
and red—and I set out to underline three different themes with a special color for each. The
themes were: covenant, sacrifice, and the shedding of blood. Blue was for covenant, green for
sacrifice, and red for the shedding of blood.

In that way, I stumbled into a revelation because I discovered that wherever I had the blue,
I had the green; and wherever I had the green,
I had the red. In other words, wherever there
is a covenant, there must be a sacrifice; and
wherever there is a sacrifice, there must be the
shedding of blood.

This agrees with the description of God's people in Psalm 50:5: *"those who cut My covenant on the basis of a sacrifice."* Two things are essential for entering into a permanent relationship with God: a covenant and a sacrifice. Without a covenant, there can be no relationship with God; without a sacrifice, there can be no covenant.

> WITHOUT A COVENANT, THERE CAN BE NO RELATIONSHIP WITH GOD; WITHOUT A SACRIFICE, THERE CAN BE NO COVENANT.

Historically, the way that men entered into covenant with God before the new covenant in Jesus Christ was very remarkable, and many people are not familiar with it. Jeremiah describes it well.

This was a period in Israel's history when the nation was backslidden and rebellious in their relationship to God, and they had done something God forbade them to do—they had made slaves out of their fellow Israelites. When God reproved them for this through the prophet Jeremiah, they made a show of repentance and entered into a covenant in which they agreed to release their slaves. But then, to add to their sin, they broke their covenant and took the slaves back. The only part of this incident that concerns us just now is the procedure by which they entered into the covenant. This has a significance that goes far beyond this particular moment in the history of Israel. It is described in Jeremiah, where God says,

> *And I will give the men who have transgressed My covenant, who have not fulfilled the words of the covenant which they made before Me, when they cut the calf in two and passed between its parts—the officials of Judah, and the officials of Jerusalem, the court officers, and the priests, and all the people of the land, who passed between the parts of the calf—and I will give them into the hand of their enemies.* (Jeremiah 34:18–20)

This provides an important addition to our understanding of the process of making a covenant. Not merely did making a covenant require a sacrifice, but the sacrifice also had to be dealt with in a special way. The animal that was killed as the sacrifice was cut into two parts, and the two parts were placed opposite one another with a space in between. Then the people who were making the covenant passed between the two parts of the sacrifice. This was the act by which they entered into the covenant.

God's Covenant with Abram

Keeping in mind this procedure for making a covenant, we'll turn to Genesis 15:7–18, which describes how the Lord entered into a covenant with Abram (his name had not yet become Abraham):

> *And He said to him, "I am the LORD who brought you out of Ur of the Chaldeans, to give you this land to possess it." And he said, "O Lord GOD, how may I know that I shall possess it?" So He said to him, "Bring Me a three year old heifer, and a three year old female goat, and a three year old ram, and a turtledove, and a young pigeon." Then he brought all these to Him and cut them in two, and laid each half opposite the other; but he did not cut the birds. And the birds of prey came down upon the carcasses, and Abram drove them away. Now when the sun was going down, a deep sleep*

fell upon Abram; and behold, terror and great darkness fell upon him. And God said to Abram, "Know for certain that your descendants will be strangers in a land that is not theirs, where they will be enslaved and oppressed four hundred years. But I will also judge the nation whom they will serve; and afterward they will come out with many possessions. And as for you, you shall go to your fathers in peace, you shall be buried at a good old age. Then in the fourth generation they shall return here, for the iniquity of the Amorite is not yet complete." And it came about when the sun had set, that it was very dark, and behold, there appeared a smoking oven and a flaming torch which passed between these pieces. On that day the LORD made a covenant with Abram, saying, "To your descendants I have given this land."

(Genesis 15:7–18)

The passage opens with the Lord making a promise to Abram that He will give him the land of Canaan for his possession. Abram responded with a question: *"How may I know...?"* In reply, the Lord proceeded to make a covenant with

Abram. In other words, God's final commitment to do anything is in a covenant. When God has entered into a covenant, there is no more that He can do to commit Himself. Covenant represents final, irrevocable commitment. Once God had made the covenant with Abram, He no longer spoke in the future tense. He did not say, "I will give," He said, *"I have given."* The covenant has settled it—finally and forever.

COVENANT REPRESENTS FINAL, IRREVOCABLE COMMITMENT.

The procedure by which the Lord entered into the covenant with Abram corresponds exactly to that described in Jeremiah 34:18–20. Abram had to take the sacrificial animals, kill them, and divide them into two pieces. Then it appears that, in due course, the Lord and Abram passed between the pieces of the sacrifice. By that strange act, the Lord entered into a covenant commitment with Abram.

Now let us look at some of the details of this transaction. Every one of them is illuminating. Genesis 15:11 reads: *"And the birds of prey came down upon the carcasses, and Abram drove them away."* These words bring back very vivid memories to me.

During World War II, while serving with the British forces in Egypt, I lay in the hospital for one full year, sick with a condition that the doctors were not able to heal. In desperation, I turned to the Bible to see what it had to say. Ultimately, after reading the whole Bible through, I came to the conclusion that God had provided healing for me through the death of Jesus Christ on the cross, that it was a part of the covenant God had made with me through Christ. But as I sought to lay hold of this truth, my mind was continually assailed with all sorts of fits of depression, doubt, and darkness.

As I lay there, wrestling to appropriate my covenant benefits in Christ and fighting off these moods of depression and doubt, I happened to read this passage in Genesis, chapter 15, and I saw that it was Abram's job to drive the birds of prey away. God ordained the sacrificial objects, but to keep them intact was Abram's job. Likewise, I saw that God had provided the sacrifice in Christ for me, but it was my job to keep those satanic birds from preying on the sacrifice and robbing me of my benefits. So I saw there was a period in which I would have to keep driving the birds away. No matter how many times doubt or unbelief or fear would attack me, it was my privilege and my responsibility to keep those sacrificial objects intact. They were not to be desecrated by the satanic birds of prey that wanted to feed on them and take away from my inheritance.

Then it says in verse 12 of Genesis, chapter 15, *"Now when the sun was going down, a deep sleep fell upon Abram; and behold, terror and great darkness fell upon him."* This was a very profound spiritual experience in which Abram, as a mature, committed believer, went through *"terror and great darkness."*

DO YOU KNOW THAT SOME OF THE GREATEST SAINTS OF GOD GO THROUGH PERIODS OF SPIRITUAL DARKNESS?

Does your theology make room for that? Do you know that some of the greatest saints of God go through periods of spiritual darkness? It is not necessarily a mark of immaturity or weakness to go through darkness. In fact, God cannot trust the immature and weak with that kind of experience. He knows just how much each one of us can endure. Abram did not go through the darkness because he was weak or uncommitted, but he went through it because it was part of his total spiritual experience. His darkness was a preview of what his descendants were to suffer in Egypt. As their father, he had to share a measure of their suffering.

In verses 13 through 16, the Lord explained to Abram what was going to happen to his descendants in Egypt, and how ultimately He would intervene and deliver them and bring them back to the land of Canaan. Then, in verse 17, a new dimension was added to Abram's experience: *"And it came about when the sun had set, that it was very dark, and behold, there appeared a smoking oven and a flaming torch which passed between these pieces."* To the normal darkness of night was added the blackness of smoke belching from an oven. Frequently, in Scripture, an oven or a furnace typifies intense suffering. In Isaiah 48:10, God said to Israel, *"Behold, I have refined you, but not as silver; I have tested you in the furnace of affliction."*

This applies at times to all of God's people. If you should ever find yourself in the furnace, remember that is where God refines you and tests you. How you react in the furnace will determine your destiny. You are not necessarily in the furnace because you are weak or backslidden or because you have failed God. You are in the furnace because the furnace does things for you that nothing else can do. In Malachi 3:3, God warned the sons of Levi, His priests, that He would refine them as gold and silver are refined. Precious metals are never purified without intense heat.

> HOW YOU REACT IN GOD'S REFINING FURNACE WILL DETERMINE YOUR DESTINY.

In the midst of this overwhelming darkness to which Abram was subjected—a darkness that was both natural and supernatural—there was *"a flaming torch which passed between these pieces"* (Genesis 15:17). What a depth of meaning there is in that! The flaming torch was a manifestation of the Spirit of God, corresponding to the *"seven lamps of fire… which are the seven Spirits of God"* (Revelation 4:5) that John saw before the throne in heaven. It was at this moment—the moment of deepest darkness—that the Lord, in the appearance of the flaming torch, made His commitment to

Abram. He passed between the pieces and, in so doing, He entered into the covenant.

Let me return again for a moment to my experience in the hospital in Egypt. It was at that time of darkness in my own life that the truth of this incident in Genesis, chapter 15, became so vivid to me. I learned that there are times of utter darkness when the Holy Spirit will illuminate only one thing, the emblems of the sacrifice, because that is all we need to see. The sacrifice is the emblem of the covenant, and the covenant is God's final, irrevocable commitment.

You may pass through a time when you can see nothing but the one fact that Jesus died for you. That is all you need to know. Everything is included in that. Romans 8:32 tells us, *"He who did not spare His own Son, but delivered Him up for us all, how will He not also with Him freely give us all things?"* There are times when that is all you can hold on to. It is the covenant made in the sacrificial death of the Lord Jesus Christ.

That is how the Lord and Abram entered into covenant. As I understand it, each passed in turn between the pieces of the sacrifices. Isn't it amazing that almighty God would do that with a man? It staggers my mind that, in a certain sense, God would come all the way down from heaven to pass between those pieces of slain animals to make His commitment to Abram. I am overwhelmed to realize that God would go to such lengths to make His personal commitment to a man.

Valid Only Through Death

But why was a sacrifice necessary? Why was that the only way to enter into a covenant? The answer is that the sacrifice symbolized the death of each party to the covenant. As each party walked between the pieces of the slain animal, he was saying, in effect, "That is my death. That animal died as my representative. He died in my place. As I enter into this covenant, I enter by death. Now that I am in covenant, I have no more right to live." That explains why both Hebrew and Greek make no distinction between *covenant* and *testament*.

The necessity of death to make a covenant valid is emphasized in Hebrews:

> *For where a covenant is, there must of necessity be the death of the one who made it. For a covenant is valid only when men are dead, for it is never in force while the one who made it lives.*
>
> (Hebrews 9:16–17)

These words leave no room for misunderstanding. The one who enters into a covenant enters into it by death. As long as a person remains alive, he is not in covenant. It is impossible to be in covenant and remain alive. The death of the sacrificed animal is physical, but it symbolizes another form of death for the one who offers the sacrifice and passes through the pieces. The one who does this hereby renounces all right, from that moment, to live for himself. As each party passes through the pieces of the sacrifice, he says, in effect, to the other, "If need be, I will die for you. From now on, your interests take precedence over my own. If I have anything you need but cannot supply, then my supply becomes your supply. I no longer live for myself; I live for you."

In God's sight, this act of making a covenant is no empty ritual. It is a solemn and sacred commitment. If we trace through history the course of events that resulted from the Lord's covenant with Abram, we see that each party had to make good on the commitment that the covenant represented.

Some years later, when Abram had become Abraham, God said to him, "I want your son Isaac, your only son. The most precious thing you have is no longer yours, because you and I are in covenant. It is mine." To his eternal credit, Abraham did not falter. He was willing to offer up even Isaac. Only at the last moment did the Lord intervene directly from heaven and stop him from actually slaying his son. (See Genesis 22.)

ON THE CROSS, JESUS LAID DOWN HIS LIFE AS THE FULL PRICE OF REDEMPTION FOR ABRAHAM AND ALL HIS DESCENDANTS.

However, that is not the end of the story. God had also committed Himself to Abraham. Two thousand years later, God, in His turn, fulfilled His part of the covenant. To meet the need of Abraham and his descendants, God offered up His only Son. But this time, there was no last minute reprieve. On the cross, Jesus laid down His life as the full price of redemption for Abraham and all his descendants. That act was the outcome of the commitment that God and Abram had made to each other on that fateful night, two thousand years earlier, when they passed between those pieces of the sacrifice. All that followed from then on in the course of history was determined by their covenant.

As a matter of fact, the whole of history is the outworking of God's covenant, which explains a lot of what is happening in the Middle East. The Jewish people were restored to Israel because God promised it to them four thousand years ago. He gave it to them in covenant, and God is not a covenant-breaker.

The commitment that is made in a covenant is that solemn, that total, and that irrevocable.

THREE

Union between Man and Woman

Chapter 3

Union between Man and Woman

In the first chapter, we saw that marriage on the highest plane is *"a cord of three strands"* (Ecclesiastes 4:12)—a covenant between a man, a woman, and God. In chapter 2, we discovered that a covenant requires a sacrifice; otherwise it is not valid. In this chapter, we will apply these principles specifically to a marriage in which believers are united through their faith in Christ.

The sacrifice upon which the covenant of Christian marriage is based is the death of Jesus Christ on our behalf. He is the sacrifice through which, by faith, a man and a woman can pass into the relationship of marriage as God Himself ordained that it should be. Just as the Lord and Abram passed between the pieces of the slain animals, so in marriage a man and woman pass through the death of Jesus Christ on their behalf into a totally new life and a totally new relationship that would have been impossible without the death of Jesus Christ. The covenant of Christian marriage is made at the foot of the cross.

There are three successive phases in the outworking of this relationship. First, a life is laid down. Each lays down his life for the other. The husband looks back at Christ's death on the cross and says, "That death was my death. When I came through the cross, I died. Now I am no longer living for myself." The wife likewise looks at the cross and says the same, "That death was my death. When I came through the cross, I died. Now I am no longer living for myself."

Henceforth, each holds nothing back from the other. Everything the husband has is for the wife. Everything the wife has is for the husband. No reservations, nothing held back. It is a merger, not a partnership.

Second, out of that death comes a new life. Each now lives out that new life in and through the other. The husband says to the wife, "My life is in you. I am living out my life through you. You are the expression of what I am." Likewise, the wife says to the husband, "My life is in you. I am living out my life through you. You are the expression of what I am."

Third, the covenant is consummated by physical union. This in turn brings forth fruit, which continues the new life that each has been willing to share with the other. In the whole realm of living creatures, God has ordained this basic principle: Without union, there can be no fruit. Covenant leads to shared life and fruitfulness; life that is not shared remains sterile and fruitless.

COVENANT LEADS TO SHARED LIFE AND FRUITFULNESS; LIFE THAT IS NOT SHARED REMAINS STERILE AND FRUITLESS.

This approach to marriage, which sees it in terms of a covenant, is very different from the attitude with which most people today enter into marriage. Basically, the attitude of our contemporary culture is, "What can I get? What is there in this for me?" I believe that any relationship approached with this attitude is doomed to end in failure. The one who approaches marriage as a covenant does not ask, "What can I get?" Rather he asks, "What can I give?" And he goes on to answer his own question: "I give my life. I lay it down for you, and then I find my new life in you." This applies equally to each party—to the husband and to the wife. To the natural mind, this sounds ridiculous. Yet it is, in fact, the secret of real life, real happiness, and real love.

> IN SOME SENSE, THE WIFE IS THE PIVOT UPON WHICH THE WHOLE RELATIONSHIP TURNS.

In 1 Samuel 25, Scripture records the story of a woman named Abigail, who became David's second wife. When he met her, she was living in the hills of Judea with her husband Nabal. Nabal means "fool," and it wasn't long before he was dead as a result of his foolishness. David sent messengers to ask her if she'd marry him, and she sent back a message that has always gripped my heart. She said, *"Behold, your maidservant is a maid to wash the feet of my lord's servants"* (1 Samuel 25:41). How many of you would be able to say something that self-sacrificing?

In this new relationship of self-sacrifice, each party has a special contribution to make. It is noteworthy that in every passage of the New Testament that deals with the mutual obligations of husband and wife, the writer always began by explaining the special responsibilities of the wife. This is true whether the writer was Peter (a married man) or Paul (an unmarried man). It would seem that, in some sense, the wife is the pivot upon which the whole relationship turns. Unless she plays her part, there is no way that the husband on his own can make the relationship work. We will begin, therefore, by looking at the wife's contribution.

The Wife's Contribution

In Proverbs 31:10–31, Solomon painted one of the most beautiful portraits to be found anywhere in the Bible, that of an *"excellent wife."* The King James Version translates this *"a virtuous woman."* Neither translation fully expresses the force of the original. What Solomon really had in mind, I believe, is a woman who knows what it is to be a woman—a woman who knows how to make the fullest and richest expression of her womanhood, a woman who succeeds as a woman.

He opened his description with a question: *"An excellent wife, who can find?"* (Proverbs 31:10). This would indicate that such a woman is rare. Since I was privileged to share thirty years of my life with a woman who answered to Solomon's description, I can never read this passage without tears of gratitude coming into my eyes.

It is outside the scope of this book to examine every detail of the portrait that Solomon painted. But I want to point out one simple fact that is very significant: the beginning, the middle, and the end of the picture all focus on her husband. In other words, the supreme achievement of an excellent wife is her husband. Everything else she achieves apart from that is of secondary value. This is how a woman should measure her achievement as a wife. She is not living out her own life now. Her life is in her husband. She sees her success in him. She rejoices in his achievements more than in her own.

Notice, in verse 11, the first statement about this excellent wife: *"The heart of her husband trusts in her, and he will have no lack of gain."* He does not have to go out in the world and make himself a millionaire to prove himself. His wife's approval is sufficient for him. Many men strive unceasingly for success in business or other fields primarily out of a desire to prove themselves. Usually their root problem is that they never had the assurance of approval in their own homes—first from their parents, and later from their wives. Consequently, they go through life with a driving urge to gain approval and prove themselves. But a man who has the right kind of wife need not depend on anyone else for approval. Hers is enough. Everybody else may misunderstand him, and may even betray him, but he knows there is one person on whom he can totally rely.

> A MAN WHO HAS A SUPPORTIVE, ENCOURAGING WIFE DOES NOT NEED TO DEPEND ON ANYONE ELSE FOR APPROVAL.

That is his wife. To be a wife of this kind is a very high achievement for a woman.

The husband's trust in this *"excellent wife"* is based on one simple but vitally important fact: *"She does him good and not evil all the days of her life"* (Proverbs 31:12). For thirty years, I had that total assurance concerning Lydia. She would never do me evil. She would disagree with me, perhaps admonish me. We might argue or hold different opinions. But I always knew where I stood with her. She was 100 percent on my side. Without that, I could never have become what I am today.

Let us move on now to verse 23, the central section of this description: *"Her husband is known in the gates, when he sits among the elders of the land."* Again the focus is on her husband. He is a recognized leader among his people, sitting in the gate, the place of honor and authority. Solomon's language is so expressive. *"Her husband is known..."* In other words, he is known as her husband. Without her support, he would not have been able to hold the position of honor. This principle holds true in most cases where we see a successful, confident, respected man. A great part of what we are really seeing is his wife's success.

Then, in verses 28 and 29, the description closes with the focus on her family—first her children, but finally her husband once more:

> *Her children rise up and bless her; her husband also, and he praises her, saying: "Many daughters have done nobly, but you excel them all."* (Proverbs 31:28–29)

This description of the *"excellent wife"*—the truly successful woman—begins with, centers in, and concludes with her husband. He is her supreme achievement, beside which every other achievement is secondary.

What reward does he, on his part, have to offer her? *"He praises her."* How important that is! Husbands, if you have a wife like this, there is no salary that is adequate for her. You have nothing to pay her with except praise. And you can afford to be lavish with that form of payment because the more you pay, the more you receive in return. So take time to praise your wife. Tell her how sweet she is. Tell her how good her food tastes. Tell her how much you enjoy spending time with her. Tell her how pretty she looks. Tell her how you appreciate her wisdom and advice. Tell her how much you love her. Take time to do it. It is a good investment. You will get back many times over everything you put in.

For my part, as I have already indicated, I can look back over thirty years of happy and successful marriage with Lydia. If I have one major regret, it is that I did not tell her often enough how much I loved her. I did love her, and she knew it. But I did not tell her as often as I should have. If I could live that part of my life again, I would tell her ten times as often.

Let us return again for a moment to the wife's part. How can a wife achieve this kind of success with her husband? I would say that she has two main responsibilities, closely related to each other. The first is to uphold her husband; the second is to encourage him.

In 1 Corinthians 11:3, Paul told us that *"the man* [husband] *is the head of the woman* [wife]." In the natural body, final responsibility for decision and direction rests with the head. Yet the head cannot hold itself up. It depends upon the rest of the body to do this. Without the support of the rest of the body, primarily the neck, the head alone cannot fulfill its function.

This applies to the marriage relationship. As head, the husband has final responsibility for decision and direction. But he cannot fulfill this function on his own. He is dependent upon the body to uphold him. In a sense, the wife's responsibility may be likened to that of the neck. She is the one closest to her husband, on whose support he must continually rely. If she fails to uphold him, there is no way that he can function as he should. Just as there is no other part of the body that can take the place of the neck in upholding the head, so there is no other person who can give to the husband the support that he needs from his wife.

The wife's second main responsibility is to encourage her husband. A man should be able to look to his wife for encouragement at all times, particularly when he least deserves it. If Lydia had only encouraged me when I deserved it, it would not

THE ESSENCE OF THE MARRIAGE COVENANT IS THAT YOU ARE NO LONGER LIVING FOR YOURSELF.

have been what I needed. I needed encouragement most when I deserved it the least. I needed somebody who had faith in me when no one else did. I didn't need a sermon. I didn't need a counselor. I needed someone to trust me.

Encouraging is not an easy thing for a wife to do—especially in times of pressure. It is much easier to reproach or criticize. In fact, encouraging is a ministry that must be cultivated. I believe that many times a wife can transform a bad marriage and an unsuccessful husband into a good marriage and a successful husband if she will learn how to encourage. But that always means self-denial. We cannot encourage others when we are primarily interested in ourselves. If you and your husband are both feeling miserable, what are you going to do? Tell him how miserable you are, or encourage him? To encourage him requires self-denial. But that is the essence of the marriage covenant. You are no longer living for yourself.

This brings us back to our starting point: covenant commitment. This alone can provide the grace and the power that each party in a marriage needs to make it successful. Good advice or a set of rules are not sufficient by themselves to do this. There are a number of excellent books available today that offer counsel and instruction from a Christian viewpoint on how to have a successful marriage. But in the last resort, Christian marriage will not work without the supernatural grace of God; and this grace is received only as husband and wife yield themselves to God and to one another in covenant commitment.

The Husband's Contribution

Now we will consider the husband's contribution to the marriage covenant. A good starting place is provided by the words of Paul in 1 Corinthians 11:7: *"For a man ought not to have his head covered, since he is the image and glory of God; but the woman is the glory of man."*

It is the closing statement that we are concerned with just now, *"the woman* [wife] *is the glory of man* [husband]." This simply takes the same principle that has been applied to the wife and applies it to the husband as well. We have already seen that the wife's success was manifested in the husband. In other words, the indication that she was a successful wife is demonstrated by the fact that her husband is upheld and encouraged. Now, in verse seven, Paul is explaining that the reverse is also true—the evidence of a huband's success can be seen, or is made manifest, in his wife. She is his glory, his greatest achievement. Uniquely and supremely, she is a living demonstration of the quality of her husband. He brings out her radiance, rest and security; she encourarges and upholds. If they are successful in their roles, he is her glory, she is his.

A well-known evangelist was once asked about a fellow believer, "What kind of a Christian is he?" "I can't tell you yet," he replied, "I haven't met his wife!" That was a wise answer.

Personally, I would never form an estimate of a married man until I had come to know his wife, because she is his glory. If she is radiant and restful and secure, her husband has earned my respect. But if, on the other hand, she is frustrated and nervous and insecure, I have to conclude that there is some area of failure in the husband.

This relationship of the wife to her husband as his glory is beautifully illustrated by a parable from the heavenly bodies: the relationship of the moon to the sun. The moon is the "glory" of the sun. The moon has no glory of its own. Its only beauty comes from reflecting the radiance of the sun.

ONE RESPONSIBILITY OF A HUSBAND IS TO PROVIDE EMOTIONAL, FINANCIAL, AND SOCIAL SECURITY FOR HIS WIFE.

Some years ago, in the NASA center in Houston, Texas, I had the opportunity to see a fragment of rock from the moon's surface that had been brought back to earth by the astronauts. For a while, I gazed at it in awe. Finally, I bowed my head in reverent worship of the Creator as I began to understand the perfect wisdom of His design. The moon rock is dull and unattractive in itself. It has no brilliance or radiance of its own. Yet it is the most highly reflective material that man has yet discovered. Why? The reason, of course, is that it was designed by the Creator for one supreme purpose—to reflect the radiance of the sun. This it will continue to do, as long as nothing comes between it and the sun. But if some other body—for example, the earth—comes between the moon and the sun, the result is manifested in the moon. It loses its light.

All this is a parable that illustrates a much more wonderful work of the Creator's genius—the marriage relationship. Within a true covenant marriage, the wife is like the moon. Her greatest glory is found in her God-given purpose of reflecting her husband. When he shines on her, she glows. But if the full, open fellowship between them is broken—if something comes between them—the result is manifested in the wife. She loses her light.

Those of us who are husbands would do well to check from time to time on our performance in this regard. We should be ready to see our wife's condition as a reflection of our own. We males are often quick to notice some area of weakness in our wives—even perhaps to be unkind or critical about it. Yet it may well be that the problem we see so clearly in our wives is, in reality, the reflection of a corresponding problem that has gone unrecognized in ourselves.

What should a husband look for in his wife? What should he accept as evidence that he is fulfilling his responsibility toward her? If I had to answer this question in one word, the word I would choose would be *security*. When a married woman is truly secure—emotionally secure, financially secure, socially secure—in most cases that is sufficient evidence that her relationship with her husband is good and that he is fulfilling his obligations toward her. But if a married woman is subject to frequent or continuing insecurity, almost invariably this can be traced to one of two causes: either her husband is not fulfilling his obligation to her, or something has come in between them that prevents the wife from receiving what her husband has to give her.

What are the main practical ways in which a husband should fulfill his responsibility toward his wife? I would suggest that they can be summed up in two words: to *protect* and to *provide*.

A husband's primary practical responsibility is to protect his wife. She should feel secure. She should know that she has a covering. It is unfair to ask women to take many of the responsibilities that are thrust upon them today. They may prove to be very efficient; they may even outdo men; but they lose their femininity. In most cases, the true, underlying cause is that the husband has abdicated from his responsibility to protect his wife. A wife should always know that she has someone to stand between her and

> A WIFE NEEDS TO KNOW THAT SHE HAS SOMEONE TO STAND BETWEEN HER AND EVERY BLOW, EVERY ATTACK, EVERY PRESSURE.

every blow, every attack, every pressure.

A husband's second practical responsibility is to provide for his wife. Scripture is very clear about this. *"But if anyone does not provide for his own, and especially for those of his household, he has denied the faith, and is worse than an unbeliever"* (1 Timothy 5:8). The word *"provide"* has a wide application. A husband should see that there is no area of need in his wife for which he has not made provision—whether the need be physical, emotional, cultural, or spiritual.

However, one major area in which a husband is responsible to provide for his wife is that of finance. Normally, he should accept full responsibility for her financial needs.

A man who does not provide in this way when he can will almost inevitably forfeit some measure of authority in his home. It is hard to separate the earning of money from the right to make decisions about the way the money is spent. But the making of such decisions should be a function of headship.

We know, of course, that there are exceptions to this. There are husbands who become incapacitated and unable to work. In such cases, the responsibility for financial provision may fall upon the wife. The marriage vow makes allowance for such cases as this; it covers "in sickness" as well as "in health." However, it is wrong when unfortunate exceptions such as this become the normal rule.

Briefly, now, we may sum up the mutual responsibilities of husband and wife in this covenant relationship of marriage. The main responsibilities of the husband are to protect and to provide. The main responsibilities of the wife are to uphold and to encourage. However, the proper fulfillment of these responsibilities can never be achieved by mere unaided human effort or willpower. It takes something more than that; it takes the supernatural, all-sufficient grace of God. This kind of grace comes only as husband and wife together commit themselves to God and to one another in solemn, covenant relationship. It is the act of commitment that releases God's grace.

THE RESULT OF COVENANT COMMITMENT BETWEEN A MAN AND A WOMAN CAN BE SUMMED UP IN ONE WORD: *KNOWING*.

The outcome of this commitment is a new kind of life and relationship, one that can never be experienced by those who have not first met the conditions. We will go on now to examine the distinctive character of this new life.

Union Leads to Knowing

The result of covenant commitment between a man and a woman can be summed up in one word: *knowing*. A husband and a wife come to know each other in a depth and a degree that is not possible in any other way. The verb *to know* in the original language of Scripture has a meaning both wider and deeper than its English counterpart. In Genesis 4:1 (KJV), it says, *"And Adam knew Eve his wife; and she conceived, and bare Cain."* (The *New American Standard Bible* says, *"The man had relations with his wife Eve."* However, the King James retains the correct, literal meaning of the original Hebrew.) This is the first time that the word *know* is used in Scripture after the fall. It is also the first recorded occasion that a man and a woman came together in sexual union.

However, the writers of the Old Testament were usually very precise and discriminating in the way in which they used the verb *to know* to describe sexual intercourse between a man and a woman. In most cases, when a man came together with a woman in a covenant union that had the seal of God's approval, Scripture says that he *"knew"* her. But where it was an illicit relationship, one that God had not endorsed and did not approve, Scripture usually says that he *"lay with"* her. The implication is that it is possible for a man to have sexual intercourse with a woman and yet not *"know"* her. I believe that this is fully borne out in experience. Indeed, a man may have promiscuous sexual intercourse with fifty women, and yet never *know* one of them.

What, then, is the essential difference between merely "lying with" a woman and "knowing" a woman? The answer can be given in one word: *commitment*. The essence of sexual immorality is that a man and a woman seek physical and emotional satisfaction from each other, but they have not made a permanent commitment to each other.

A MAN CAN HAVE SEXUAL INTERCOURSE WITH A WOMAN AND YET NOT *"KNOW"* HER.

The pleasure that they obtain in this way is stolen. They have not paid the due price for it.

One of the greatest joys in life is to enter into an intimate relationship where you know another human being and are known yourself. Because it is so precious and so much is at risk, God has built a fence around it, and that fence is covenant.

It's very important to understand this, so I will give you an example. A young man and a young woman are students in a university. If they have sex together, God calls it immorality. But if the same young man and woman commit their lives to one another, go to the altar and say their vows, and then have sex, now God calls the same act holy and blessed. What makes the difference? Covenant.

This brings out how much importance God attaches to commitment. Sexual intercourse that is not preceded by permanent, mutual commitment is immorality. Premarital sex is the innocuous title given to it in contemporary society. *"Fornication"* is the blunt word used in Scripture. On the other hand, sexual union that is preceded by legitimate, mutual commitment is *marriage*. The difference in God's attitude toward these two relationships is clearly brought out in Hebrews 13:4: *"Let marriage be held in honor among all, and let the marriage bed be undefiled; for fornicators and adulterers God will judge."*

In this context, *"fornicators"* are to be understood as those who indulge in sexual relationships without covenant commitment. *"Adulterers"* are those who have made a marriage commitment, but then indulge in sexual relationships that violate their commitment. In both cases, the essence of the sin is a wrong attitude toward covenant commitment. Those who have sexual relations without covenant and commitment don't even begin to discover the blessing that God has created for them in real Christian marriage.

We return to God's ultimate purpose for marriage: that a man and a woman come to know each other. I suppose that only those who have been privileged to experience it can appreciate the full depth of this truth. Such knowledge between a man and a woman is neither temporary nor static. It is not merely intellectual, as we normally understand knowledge in contemporary terminology, nor is it merely sexual. It is a total, unreserved opening up of each personality to the other. It embraces every area—physical, emotional, intellectual, and spiritual. If the marriage pursues its God-ordained course, the mutual knowledge of husband and wife will become fuller and deeper as the years pass.

BECAUSE MARRIAGE IS SO WONDROUS AND SO SACRED, GOD HAS PROTECTED IT WITH HIS DEMAND FOR COVENANT COMMITMENT.

Marriage Covenant

It is my personal conviction that the greatest wonder of all God's creative achievement is expressed in human personality. Jesus taught that one human soul is worth more than the whole world. (See Mark 8:36–37.) I believe this is a true, objective evaluation. The whole created universe, in all its grandeur and greatness, is of less intrinsic worth than one human personality. The marvel of marriage is that, through it, two human personalities are permitted to know each other in all their uniqueness, permitted to explore the sacred, innermost depths of each other. For the very reason that marriage in this sense is so wondrous and so sacred, God has protected it with His demand for covenant commitment.

There are countless facets to the way in which a man and his wife may come to know one another. For instance, the very way in which they look at one another is different from the way in which they look at other people, or other people look at them. One of my favorite pastimes is watching a husband and wife when they are not aware that anyone is watching them. What I always look at is their eyes. (Someone has said that the eye is the "window of the soul.") Give me time to observe the looks that a husband

and wife exchange between themselves, and I will form a pretty accurate estimate of how successful their marriage is.

A wife has a way of looking at her husband that tells him almost everything without her saying anything in words. For instance, "It's time *you* took care of the kids." Or, "You shouldn't have spent so long talking to that other woman." Or, "If we go home now, we can have an hour together by ourselves." For this reason, Scripture indicates that a married woman should never permit herself to look at any other person in the way that she looks at her husband.

This is very vividly illustrated by an incident in the life of Abraham. Abraham was a great man of faith, but he had certain very human weaknesses. On two occasions, in order to save his own life, he was prepared to let his wife Sarah be taken into the harem of a Gentile king. He was slow to realize that divine destiny had linked him irrevocably with Sarah and could never be fulfilled through any other woman. Abraham's weakness in this respect should serve as a warning to husbands in this age.

In 1 Peter 3:7, Christian husbands are reminded that their wives are, with them, *"fellow heir*[s] *of the grace of life."* The phrase *"fellow heir"* indicates a joint inheritance, one that neither party can legally claim apart from the other. There are areas of God's inheritance for married couples that neither can enter without the other. These areas are reserved solely for couples who can move together in mutual love and harmony. This principle applies as much to Christian husbands today as it did in Abraham's relationship to Sarah.

> THE MARVEL OF MARRIAGE IS THAT, THROUGH IT, TWO HUMAN PERSONALITIES ARE PERMITTED TO EXPLORE THE SACRED, INNERMOST DEPTHS OF EACH OTHER.

The second of the two occasions on which Abraham was prepared to part with Sarah was in the court of Abimelech, king of Gerar. (See Genesis 20.) Abraham persuaded Sarah to say that she was his sister—which was true, but not the whole truth—and to conceal the fact that she was also his wife. As a result, Abimelech took her into his harem, intending to make her his wife. However, God intervened supernaturally to preserve Sarah. In a dream, He revealed to Abimelech that Sarah was really

Abraham's wife and warned him that if he took her, he would pay for it with his own life. Abimelech, who was apparently a God-fearing man, immediately returned Sarah to Abraham and compensated him with substantial gifts for the wrong that he had done.

In conclusion, however, Abimelech addressed a word of reproof and warning to Sarah: *"And unto Sarah he said, Behold, I have given thy brother a thousand pieces of silver: behold, he is to thee a covering of the eyes, unto all that are with thee, and with all other: thus she was reproved"* (Genesis 20:16 KJV). We may sum up the essence of Abimelech's reproof to Sarah in this way: "When you are married, you may never look at another man in the way that you look at your husband. He is a covering of the eyes to you." There is a way in which a woman opens up her eyes to her husband that is both scriptural and very sacred. She should never deliberately let any other man look into her eyes the way her husband does.

Obviously, there is another side to this: just as a married woman has no right to look in this way at a man who is not her husband, so a married man has no right to receive such a look from a woman who is not his wife. To his credit, it would seem that Abimelech recognized this.

At any rate, this warning given to Sarah by Abimelech expresses, in a simple but vivid way, the essence of the relationship into which a man and woman enter through the covenant of marriage. Through their covenant commitment to each other, they come to know one another in a way in which neither of them should ever know any other person and no other person should ever know either of them. The purpose of the marriage covenant is to preserve this unique and sacred knowledge between husband and wife and to keep it from being violated by any other relationship.

FOUR

Finding Your Mate

CHAPTER 4

Finding Your Mate

There are three choices of very great importance that usually face young people as they grow up: the choice of a Savior; the choice of a work in life (a career); and the choice of a partner in life (a wife or husband). If we have chosen Christ as our Savior, we should ask Him to guide us in the other two choices; and these other two choices are closely connected with each other because a husband and wife should be partners—workers together—in life. (See Genesis 2:18–25.)

Importance of Marriage

God attaches much greater importance to marriage than most Christians do today. Some of us from religious backgrounds have formed the idea that marriage is a sort of fortunate necessity because we are sexual beings and believe that we must be married before engaging in sexual relations. The majority of Christians really don't have any grasp on how valuable marriage is in the sight of God.

Another problem is that younger Christians, partly because they've seen so little to impress them in the lives of older Christians who are married, have completely failed to see the tremendous sanctity and importance of marriage. I really don't blame them. It's a tragic fact that we have millions of young people growing up today who have never seen a happy marriage.

Given the rising divorce rates, it's evident that couples do not take their wedding vows as seriously as they should. The marriage relationship, which should be the most stable, constant thing in a married person's life, can now be dissolved almost as quickly as it was formed. We are not giving marriage its fair due. We have not recognized its value and importance.

GOD ATTACHES MUCH GREATER IMPORTANCE TO MARRIAGE THAN MOST CHRISTIANS DO TODAY.

One of the things that awakened me to the value of marriage was the wedding ceremony in which I married my second wife, Ruth. Brother Charles Simpson brought a short but extremely penetrating message as the officiator of the ceremony. He pointed out that human history began with a marriage between Adam and Eve.

As I meditated on what Charles said, it began to grow in my heart and produce a new understanding. I realized that the revelation of Scripture begins with a marriage in Genesis. Jesus performed His first miracle at a marriage. The great climax of human history that God has foreordained is, once again, a marriage—the marriage supper of the Lamb.

"CHRIST LOVES US PASSIONATELY, AND HE WANTS TO BE LOVED PASSIONATELY."

I was interested recently to discover that rabbis, in commenting on the Old Testament book Song of Solomon, considered it, in some sense, the holiest book in the Bible. Yet, frankly, it's a picture of a very passionate love relationship between a man and a woman.

I remember also a quotation from *The Marechale* by James Strahan. In the book, he quoted one of William Booth's (the man who pioneered the Salvation Army) daughters as saying, "Christ loves us passionately, and He wants to be loved passionately." I don't believe we can ever speak of New Testament Christianity in any form without passion. This passion is supposed to be reflected in our marriage relationships.

If marriage was important enough to God that He used it to start history, to begin Jesus' ministry on earth, and to typify His relationship to the church, we should be careful about the person with whom we enter into this covenant.

Choosing "The One"

I believe the marriage relationship is the most important personal relationship that many of us will have, though not all of us are meant for it.

It is meant to be a lasting, true covenant in which both parties think of each other's welfare before their own. If you know you're committed to keep this kind of covenant, you should find someone who is equally committed to keeping it and working through any problems you may have together.

A Christian should always choose a Christian partner. *"Can two walk together, except they be agreed?"* (Amos 3:3 KJV).

> *Do not be bound together with unbelievers; for what partnership have righteousness and lawlessness, or what fellowship has light with darkness? Or what harmony has Christ with Belial, or what has a believer in common with an unbeliever? Or what agreement has the temple of God with idols? For we are the temple of the living God; just as God said, "I will dwell in them and walk among them; and I will be their God, and they shall be My people."*
>
> (2 Corinthians 6:14–16)

This is the Word of God, and you can't change what God's Word says just so you can do things the way you'd like to do them. The Bible can mean only what it means. You can't make it say something else.

Years ago, Germany was forbidden to rearm as a result of World War I. But, when Hitler came to power, he set to work secretly rearming the nation. He established factories, saying they were to build baby carriages, but really they were to build machine guns.

There was a man in one of these carriage factories whose wife was pregnant. He wanted a baby carriage, so he persuaded his various friends who worked in different departments to each steal a part so he could assemble them at home. His friends cooperated with him.

One day, a few of them met the man walking down the street looking perplexed. "What's the problem?" they asked.

> GOD'S PLAN FOR MARRIAGE IS FOR HIS PEOPLE TO BE EQUALLY YOKED WITH BELIEVERS.

"Well," he said, "I put it all together twice, but each time it makes a machine gun!"

That's the Bible. It makes what it was made to make. You can't make it mean something else. When Jesus laid down the conditions for covenant, that settled it. There's no other way. God's plan for marriage is for His people to be equally yoked with believers.

Here is a list of questions you can ask yourself about your potential mate to ensure that he or she is a committed Christian.

- Does he/she love God more than me?

- Does he/she love God more than self?

- Does he/she witness with assurance that he/she is born again of the Spirit of God?

- Does he/she regularly read the Bible and know what it teaches?

- Does he/she regularly attend a church where the Word of God is preached?

- Does he/she like to talk about spiritual things? *"For the mouth speaks out of that which fills the heart"* (Matthew 12:34).

- Does he/she lead a clean, pure life?

- Does he/she have a real desire to lead others to the Lord and see them saved?

- Has he/she received the baptism in the Holy Spirit?

If the answer to several of these questions is "no," then you are not choosing the right partner. If you are a Spirit-filled Christian and you marry someone who is not a real believer—and so cannot share your spiritual experiences—two things are sure to happen: first, you will have much sorrow and pain in your heart; and second, you will not be able to serve the Lord as well as you would have if you had married a true believer.

Perhaps you are thinking, "I will marry an unsaved person, and then I will persuade that person to become a Christian." But that is foolishness! Above all else, a Christian is a person who obeys God. So you are planning to disobey God by marrying an unbeliever in order to persuade that believer to obey God (by becoming a Christian). You will try to persuade that person to obey God when you yourself are disobeying God! How will that ever work?

A young lady once took a young man to see her pastor and said, "This is the young man whom I am going to marry."

"Is he a Christian?" asked the pastor.

"Not yet," said the young lady, "but I will help him to become one after we are married."

"Before you make up your mind, I would like you to do something for me," said the pastor. He pointed to a table in the room and said, "Just climb up onto that table and stand there for a moment." The young lady did so. "Now," said the pastor, "give the young man your hand, and try to lift him onto the table beside you." Then he turned to the young man and said, "Now you try to pull the young lady down to you."

Within a few moments, the young lady was down on the floor beside the young man. "That's how it will be when you are married," said the pastor. "You will not be able to pull him up to your level, but he will pull you down to his."

So it is when a Christian marries an unbeliever. It is always easier for the unsaved partner to make the Christian a backslider than for the saved partner to make the unbeliever a Christian.

Here are three things to remember when choosing your mate:

- Remember that marriage doesn't change a person's character. If a person had a bad character before marriage, that person will still have a bad character after marriage.
- Remember that marriage is for life. If you buy a bad T-shirt or an ill-fitting dress, it will wear out and you can buy another. But if you marry the wrong man or woman, you cannot change that person. You are now committed to that person as long as you both shall live.
- Remember that when you have strong feelings about a person or a thing, it is not easy to find out the will of God about that person or thing. Therefore, before your feelings become too strong for you, you should earnestly pray to

99

the Lord, "Savior, choose my partner in life for me. Perform Your will, not mine, in my life."

The Importance of Purity

One of the best things about God's provision for marriage is that, by insisting on covenant and commitment as the way to marriage, He has provided protection against anyone being exploited or betrayed.

In 1 Thessalonians 5:23, we get the Bible's revelation of the total human personality. It is contained in a prayer of Paul for the believers he is writing to:

> *Now may the God of peace Himself sanctify you entirely; and may your spirit and soul and body be preserved complete, without blame at the coming of our Lord Jesus Christ.*

Notice the words there *"entirely"* and *"complete."* Paul is talking about the total human personality and he presents it in three elements. *"May your spirit and soul and body be preserved complete."* So that's the Bible's revelation of the total human personality. It consists of three elements: the spirit and the soul, the inner nature; the body, the outward visible nature.

Any woman who allows herself to have sexual relations with a man, without that man first making a covenant commitment, is really prostituting her entire personality, her spirit, soul, and body. I am not just talking in terms of sexual morality; I am saying that, in actual fact, that woman is desecrating the most precious thing she has. She is exposing her personality to someone who is not willing to pay the price that God requires. It is the same with a man when he has relations with a woman with whom he has no covenant.

I sometimes look back on my own first marriage and think how Lydia and I were continually coming to know one another more deeply and more intimately. Our marriage grew richer and fuller the longer it lasted. Our relationship didn't just depend on how we talked with one another nor merely upon our sexual relationship; it was a total knowing of one person by another. That was an amazing gift of God to us. I pray He brings you a spouse with whom you can have this type of covenant relationship.

A Vision for the Future

I believe God should make the decision that a man needs a wife. I believe God should anoint the woman that He has appointed for the man. I believe God should bring the woman to the man. And I believe that God has to determine the purpose and nature of their relationship. Don't live below the level of God's best.

When Lydia died, it was like someone had torn out my insides. There's no way to express the agony I felt. Yet, you have to realize that if you want the good, you've got to take what goes with it. The more you love a person, the more you'll miss them when they go.

> DON'T LIVE BELOW THE LEVEL OF GOD'S BEST.

I told the Lord that I was willing to live single if I could serve Him better that way. I was perfectly sincere. After being single for about two years or so, I had come to the conclusion that I would die a widower.

In 1977, I went to Israel with a truly interesting and wonderful group of men. I decided that I would stay an extra week in Israel to seek out God's will for my future, especially to consider whether I should work again in Israel, completing my original call to that land.

In the course of that week, I went to visit a mission that distributed my literature throughout Israel in Hebrew and Arabic and many other languages. I'd received a letter from a brother in charge of the mission, and at the bottom, his secretary had added a little note in handwriting, "Your ministry means so much to me." So, I thought I'd also do the courtesy of seeing this secretary and expressing my appreciation. I try to show my gratefulness to people who show me any kind of kindness.

When I got to the headquarters, they said the secretary had injured her back and was at home in her apartment. I looked at David Rose, who had come with me, and thought, *If there's one thing I am successful at, it is praying for people with injured backs.* I told him, "If you like, David, you and I can go and pray for her."

They told us the address, and David and I promptly got lost in Jerusalem. He was driving the van, and I said, "David, let's give up. God probably doesn't want us here." Right at that moment, we realized we were outside the secretary's home.

We went in, and there was Ruth, lying on the couch. David and I talked with her for a bit and then prayed for her. She'd had a spinal curvature for many, many years. She also had a ruptured disc. Although that was not healed at that time, it has been healed since. It was a good visit, and I was glad we'd been able to pray for her.

On my last day in Israel, I went to bed and had the most unusual night of my life. I got up at six in the morning, and I had not slept one wink. All night the Lord had dealt with me about His purposes for my life, His calling, and the promises that He'd given me. He said very clearly, "Every promise I've ever given you will be fulfilled if you believe in Me and obey Me." Then I had a vision.

I saw the zigzag road back to Jerusalem that goes up to the old city at the southwest corner. I felt that it was leading me to where I was supposed to be. Strangely, right at the beginning of the road there was this woman sitting in a green dress. I knew the woman was the secretary I had visited and prayed for. God made it clear to me that the first step in my return to Jerusalem was to marry that woman. I don't know what you think my reaction was, but I tell you, I was upset. I thought, *Lord, I don't love that woman. Are You asking me to marry someone I don't love?*

I decided not to say anything about this to anyone. Instead I prayed about it for one month. The more I prayed, the more I became convinced that this was the will of God.

I thought I'd better do something about it, so I wrote a letter to the lady telling her she should visit David Rose's fellowship in Kansas City if she ever came to America. She received the letter three days before she was set to leave for the United States!

"EVERY PROMISE I'VE EVER GIVEN YOU WILL BE FULFILLED IF YOU BELIEVE IN ME AND OBEY ME."

So, we met in Kansas City. The Lord opened a way for us to spend some time together in David Rose's home, and one evening, just before we were going to have a meeting, Ruth came to my room and said, "I want to speak with you. I need your counsel."

Because she still had a ruptured disc, she didn't like sitting in a chair, so she sat on the floor and leaned against the wall. As she sat there, I saw her in exactly the position that God had showed me in the vision. When she began to talk to me, an overwhelming love for her came over me. I mean, it was like electricity! I was sorely tempted to tell her everything. However, I didn't want to scare her. Besides, as a well-known preacher, I thought I should get some more counsel before jumping into anything.

Ruth's visit came to an end. She was going back to Israel; I was going to South Africa. I'd planned to make a stopover in Jerusalem just for a rest. So we made plans to meet in Israel for Yom Kippur. By this time, the Lord had begun speaking to her, too. Without my saying anything to her, He showed her that He wanted her to marry me.

When we met again, I told Ruth what the Lord had shown me about her. We talked for hours and hours. Over the course of two days, I fell deeply in love with her. She was God's gift to me.

Now, I'm not saying that you can't get married unless you have a vision. It doesn't happen like that for everyone. But you do need to be sure that the one you choose is the one God has chosen for you. You need to let God be your matchmaker. If He led me to the right woman twice in one lifetime, He can certainly lead you to your future spouse.

Two Together

Two are better than one because they have a good return for their labor. For if either of them falls, the one will lift up his companion. But woe to the one who falls when there is not another to lift him up. Furthermore, if two lie down together they keep warm, but how can one be warm alone? And if one can over-power him who is alone, two can resist him. (Ecclesiastes 4:9–12)

That's very down-to-earth isn't it? Marriage, aside from being a beautiful illustration of God's covenant relationship with us, is very practical.

A spouse is a beautiful gift from God—a sort of God-sanctioned support system that makes living this life easier.

Trust God to lead you to your Proverbs 31 woman. She's out there. He led me to two such women in my lifetime! And there are many godly men, too.

In the meantime, focus on becoming the man or woman God wants you to be, so you can be a blessing to your future spouse. Next to my life in Christ, the greatest blessing in my life has been the privilege of being married to two industrious, capable, intelligent women.

I didn't find these women myself. When it comes to intellectual understanding, I'm above the average. But, when it comes to judging people, I have a hard time discerning a person's true character. I thank God for never permitting me to make my own choice of a wife. In each occasion, He showed me specifically and clearly exactly whom I was to marry.

FOCUS ON BECOMING THE MAN OR WOMAN GOD WANTS YOU TO BE, SO YOU CAN BE A BLESSING TO YOUR FUTURE SPOUSE.

Now, as I said before, God may not give you a vision, as He did for me. But I do know that God has given you the guidelines you need to make a good choice. I pray that you will be led by the Holy Spirit and the teaching of God's Word in every relationship decision you make. Remember, God created man and woman, invented marriage, and was the first matchmaker. Entrust this area of your life to Him, whether He means you for marriage or not, and you will not be disappointed.

FIVE

Union with God

CHAPTER 5

Union with God

The marriage covenant is not merely sacred in its own right. It is sacred also because it typifies other relationships of great spiritual significance. The first and the most important of these is the relationship that God desires to have with His people.

God, the Husband of His People

In various passages of the Old Testament, God compared His relationship with Israel to that of a husband with a wife. He traced this relationship back to the covenant that He made with Israel at Mount Sinai after He had delivered them out of Egypt. Thus, God's relationship as a husband to Israel, like the human relationship of a man with his wife, is based on a covenant that He entered into when He made them His people. This is clearly brought out in Jeremiah:

> *"Behold, days are coming," declares the* LORD, *"when I will make a new covenant with the house of Israel and with the house of Judah, not like the covenant which I made with their fathers in the day I took them by the hand to bring them out of the land of Egypt, My covenant which they broke, although I was a husband to them," declares the* LORD.
> (Jeremiah 31:31–32)

God said that when He brought Israel out of Egypt and made a covenant with them, He entered into the relationship of a husband to them by that act. However, by unfaithfulness and idolatry, Israel violated the covenant and forfeited her right to this relationship with God as their husband. Nevertheless, rather than finally rejecting Israel for her unfaithfulness, God declared that, at the close of this age, He would make a new covenant with the Israelites, and thus once again become their husband.

In the third chapter of Hosea, we again find God's relationship with Israel pictured as that of a husband to his wife:

> *Then the* LORD *said to me, "Go again, love a woman who is loved by her husband, yet*

an adulteress, even as the LORD loves the
sons of Israel, though they turn to other
gods and love raisin cakes." (Hosea 3:1)

By his continuing love for his wife, Gomer, in spite of her unfaithfulness, the prophet Hosea becomes a metaphor of God's continuing love for Israel, as Israel's husband, which does not cease even though the Israelites have been persistently unfaithful on their side of the relationship.

In Hosea as in Jeremiah, there is a prophetic promise that God will eventually bring Israel back into covenant with Himself and thereby restore His relationship to them as their husband.

"And it will come about in that day," de-
clares the LORD, "that you will call Me
Ishi [my Husband] *and will no longer*
call Me Baali [my Master]." (Hosea 2:16)

Then, in verse 18, God spoke of the new covenant that He would make with them. In verses 19 and 20, He pictured the result of this covenant as the restoration of His marriage relationship to them:

And I will betroth you to Me forever; yes,
I will betroth you to Me in righteousness

113

and in justice, in lovingkindness and in compassion, and I will betroth you to Me in faithfulness. Then you will know the LORD. (Hosea 2:19–20)

There is special significance in the closing statement of verse 20: *"Then you will know the* LORD." We have already seen that, in the natural, covenant brings a man and a woman into a union in which they come to know each other as they never could without such a commitment. Here the principle is applied to Israel's restored relationship to God. Through their covenant commitment they will come to *"know the* LORD" as they have never known Him before.

CHRIST SANTIFIES HIS CHURCH SO THAT HE MAY PRESENT IT AS A BRIDE IS PRESENTED TO HER HUSBAND.

Briefly, then, we may sum up the Old Testament picture of God's relationship to Israel as follows: The covenant that God made with Israel at Mount Sinai is viewed as establishing a marriage relationship between God and Israel, through which He became her husband. Subsequently, through unfaithfulness and idolatry, Israel violated the covenant and forfeited her right to this relationship. God did not finally reject Israel on this account, nor did His love for her cease. Therefore, His ultimate purpose is to establish a new covenant with the Israelites through which He will once again enter into the relationship of a husband to her people. This new covenant, unlike the first, will be eternal. It will never be violated. Through it, Israelites will come to know the Lord with a totally new depth of intimacy such as they have never hitherto experienced.

The New Testament more fully unveils the nature of this new covenant. It is based not on the sacrifice of animals, but on the atoning death of Jesus Christ, the Son of God. This is the covenant into which all those, of whatever race or background, who acknowledge Jesus as Savior and Lord have already entered. Consistent with the pattern already established in the Old Testament, this new covenant in Christ is viewed as bringing believers into a relationship with God that is analogous to the marriage relationship between husband and wife.

In Ephesians 5:25–33, Paul said that Christ redeems and sanctifies His church so that He may present it to Himself as a bride is presented to her husband, *"holy and blameless"* (v. 27). Paul went on to apply this truth in a practical way to the natural relationship between husband and wife, but he closed by saying, *"This mystery is great; but I am speaking with reference to Christ and the church."* In other words, the relationship between Christ and the church is analogous to that between a husband and his wife.

One Spirit with God

In 1 Corinthians, Paul applied this picture not merely to the relationship of God to His people as a whole, but also to the relationship that God desires to have with each individual believer:

> *Or do you not know that the one who joins himself to a harlot is one body with her? For He says, "The two will become one flesh." But the one who joins himself to the Lord is one spirit with Him.*
>
> (1 Corinthians 6:16–17)

As usual with the writers of Scripture, Paul was very frank. He was speaking about the sexual union between a man and a woman. He said that a man who has sexual relations with a harlot makes himself one body with her. Then he went on to say that a believer can have a similar kind of union with God in which he becomes one spirit with God. Plus, the relationship that God invites each believer to have with Him is precisely parallel, on the spiritual plane, to the sexual union that, on the physical plane, a man may have with a woman.

In chapter three, we have already seen the essential difference between the marriage union, which is pure and holy, and fornication, which is sinful. The difference is that the marriage union is preceded by mutual covenant commitment on the part of the man and the woman. In fornication, on the other hand, a man and a woman seek sexual satisfaction from each other without being willing to make a covenant commitment to each other.

THERE IS NO WAY TO THE INTIMACY OF UNION WITH GOD, WHICH IS GODLINESS, EXCEPT THROUGH COVENANT COMMITMENT.

The language Paul used in 1 Corinthians 6:16–17 clearly justifies us in applying this principle also to the relationship between God and the believer. God desires spiritual union with each believer. At the same time, however, it is certain that God will never violate His own laws. He will never be a party to "spiritual fornication." Therefore, union with God in this sense depends upon, and must be preceded by, covenant commitment to God. Until a believer is ready to make the total, unreserved commitment to God that covenant requires, he can never have this full spiritual union with God, which is the purpose of redemption.

Earlier, in examining Psalm 50:5, we saw how God defines His *"godly ones"* as those "who cut a covenant with Him on the basis of a sacrifice." The lesson is the same as that of 1 Corinthians 6:16–17. There is no way to the intimacy of union with God, which is godliness, except through covenant commitment. Without such commitment, a person can never truly be a "godly one." He can never be truly united with God.

The Door and the Shepherd

The only pathway to a true relationship with Christ, then, is through the covenant of His sacrifice. Are we willing? Are we ready? Are we prepared to go the way of the cross?

God created us with a legitimate desire for Him, but some of us are trying to fulfill that desire illegitimately.

I am the door; if anyone enters through Me, he shall be saved, and shall go in and out, and find pasture. The thief comes only to steal, and kill, and destroy; I came that they might have life, and might have it abundantly. I am the good shepherd; the good shepherd lays down His life for the sheep. (John 10:9–11)

How can Jesus be both the door and the shepherd? Have you ever stopped to examine how both those statements can be true? There's actually a very simple solution. I believe that Jesus crucified is the door—and there is no other door—and Jesus resurrected is the shepherd.

If you want the resurrected Jesus as your shepherd, you've got to go through the door, which is the crucified Jesus. There is no other way.

Now Jesus said that a lot of people—the thieves and robbers—try to climb up some other way. They're stealing. They're trying to lay claim to blessings and provisions that they're not entitled to.

This explains the pathetic condition of many people in our churches today. They desire a relationship with God. They may even lay claim to such a relationship. Nevertheless, their desire is unfulfilled; their claim is unjustified. The reason is that they have never made that solemn, unreserved, personal commitment to God through Christ, which is the only basis upon which He will receive them into the relationship that they desire.

Such people may indeed have "made a decision" at an evangelistic campaign. They may have gone forward in a church and shaken the pastor by the hand. They may even have gone through a religious ritual, such as baptism or confirmation. But all these acts—and many others too numerous to list—are of no avail unless they bring people into a vital, committed, covenant relationship with God. Short of this, there can be no true intimacy with God. He does not commit Himself to the uncommitted.

Life's Purpose Is Knowing God

For those, however, who are willing to enter into this type of covenant commitment to God, the reward is great. It is beautifully expressed by the words that Jesus addressed to the Father in John 17:3: *"And this is eternal life, that they may know Thee, the only true God, and Jesus Christ whom Thou hast sent."* I once heard a paraphrase that rendered the verse, *"And this is* [the purpose] *of eternal life, that they may know Thee, the only true God."* Here, indeed, is the ultimate purpose of all life—to know the one true God. Out of this knowledge there comes eternal life, divine life, the life of God Himself, shared with the believer.

Again, knowledge of this kind is not merely intellectual. It is not merely theology or doctrine. It is not knowing about God. It is actually knowing God Himself—knowing Him directly and intimately, knowing Him as a Person. It is a person-to-person relationship. It is a spiritual union.

> THE ULTIMATE PURPOSE OF ALL LIFE IS TO KNOW THE ONE TRUE GOD.

Knowing God in this way is exactly parallel, on the spiritual plane, to the way in which a man may come to "know" a woman as his wife, and a woman may come to "know" a man as her husband. The use in Scripture of the same word to describe each type of relationship is no accident. It reveals the deep, underlying similarity that exists between the two relationships. As we saw earlier, in the natural, a man and a woman can never truly "know" one another unless they first make an unreserved, covenant commitment to each other. Likewise, in the spiritual, a believer can never truly "know" God unless he has first made an unreserved, covenant commitment to God. The same principle applies on each plane: Without covenant there can be no union; and without commitment there can be no covenant.

Does commitment of this kind sound too intense for you? Too intimate? Too absolute? In the last resort, each of us must make his own decision about this. But let me say that, for myself, I could never be interested in some watered-down, religious substitute for the real thing. Rather, I echo the words of David:

> *O God, Thou art my God; I shall seek Thee earnestly; my soul thirsts for Thee, my flesh yearns for Thee, in a dry and weary land where there is no water.*
>
> (Psalm 63:1)

To the soul who is truly thirsty, there can be only one source of ultimate satisfaction: it is God Himself. To stop at less than true union with Him is to miss the real purpose of living.

It is to remain forever frustrated, forever unfulfilled.

In Isaiah 1:22, God told rebellious, backslidden Israel, *"Your silver has become dross, your drink diluted with water."* The same could be said to many churches today. They have lost their purity, their true character. We are asked to accept something adulterated and impure, a cheap counterfeit of the real thing.

In the natural, if somebody were to offer me wine diluted with water, my response would be, "Spare yourself the trouble; keep the whole thing!" But today in the society and in too many churches, we are mixing everything with water. We dilute it, we water it down, we lower the standards. Our silver no longer has its proper value; our wine no longer has its proper flavor.

In such a spiritual climate, it takes a person of considerable strength of character to settle for nothing less than God's best. Such a person must be willing to say, "Others may do it the way they please, but I will do it God's way. I want a real relationship with God. I want a marriage that works, a home that glorifies God, and children who grow up happy and secure. Yes, I want these things—and I am willing to pay the price!"

Marriage Covenant

God has made the price quite clear: it is a covenant commitment—on the vertical plane, to God Himself; on the horizontal plane, to our mates.

SIX

Union with God's People

CHAPTER 6

Union with God's People

I n the preceding chapters, we have seen that covenant is the indispensable condition for true union. In chapter 3, we saw how this principle applies to the union between a man and a woman, which we call marriage. In chapter 5, we saw how it applies also to the union of each believer with God, which on the spiritual plane is analogous to the marriage union. In this chapter, we will examine how the same principle applies to yet another relationship of vital importance: the relationship of God's people to one another.

Covenant Makes a "People"

In the Old Testament, we find that, from the time God entered into a covenant with Abraham, Abraham's descendants (through the line of Isaac and Jacob) were set apart from all other members of the human race. They were known as *"the seed of Abraham"* (2 Chronicles 20:7 KJV). However, the outworking of God's purpose required that the covenant be established a second time, not with Abraham individually, but with all his descendants collectively. This took place at Mount Sinai after the Exodus. Thereafter, they were designated by a new title in the singular form: a *people* (Hebrew *'am*). This indicated that through entering into the covenant they had become a new, collective unit.

The process by which God entered into His covenant with Israel is described in Exodus, beginning in chapter 19. Here, God declared the purpose for which He was bringing Israel into covenant relationship with Himself:

> *Now then, if you will indeed obey My voice and keep My covenant, then you shall be My own possession among all the peoples, for all the earth is Mine; and you shall be to Me a kingdom of priests and a holy nation.* (Exodus 19:5–6)

We need to understand that, from then on, Israel was set apart unto God as a special people, not by any intrinsic righteousness of their own, but by the covenant God made with them. It is important to see that their holiness was the outcome of the covenant, not the reason for it. To express this another way: God did not enter into a covenant with Israel because they were holy; rather, He made them holy by entering into a covenant with them.

In the preceding chapter, we saw that, on the basis of this covenant, God assumed toward them the relationship and the responsibility of a husband. The covenant established a relationship between God and Israel analogous to that between a husband and a wife. It gave her a unique relationship to God in the same way that marriage gives a woman a unique relationship to her husband.

However, the only basis on which Israel had a right to continue in this unique and special relationship with God was by remaining faithful to the covenant. For this reason, God prefixed the declaration of His purpose for them by the word *if*. *"If you will indeed obey My voice and keep My covenant, then you shall be My own possession among all the peoples...and a holy nation"* (Exodus 19:5–6, emphasis added). Israel's continuing unique relationship to God was, therefore, bound up with their abiding by the terms of the covenant. This is why, when Israel lapsed into idolatry, their prophets frequently categorized their sin as adultery. It was analogous to that of a wife who had failed to abide by her marriage commitment to her husband.

From the time that God established this covenant with Israel, a careful distinction was made by the Old Testament writers in their usage of two related Hebrew words: *goy* (na-tion) and *'am* (people). All nations, including Israel, are *goyim* (plural of *goy*)—"*nations.*" But Israel alone is also *'am*—a "*people.*" That which singles Israel out by this distinctive title from all other nations is her unique covenant relationship with God.

> IT TAKES A COVENANT (*B'RIT*) TO CONSTITUTE A PEOPLE (*'AM*).

In the New Testament, the same distinction is maintained by the use of two different Greek words: *ethnos* (nation), which corresponds to the Hebrew *goy*, and *laos* (people), which corresponds to the Hebrew *'am*. The Greek *ethnos*, in its plural form *ethne*, is translated alternatively "*nations*" or "*Gentiles.*" It is important to understand that the word *Gentiles* normally does not refer to people who are not Christians, but rather refers to people who are not Israelites.

This analysis of the distinctive words used both in Hebrew and in Greek for *"people"* and *"nations"* has been necessary to establish one vital basic principle of Scripture: It takes a covenant (*b'rit*) to constitute a people (*'am*). An ethnic group that has no collective covenant with God is merely a "nation," but an ethnic group that has a collective covenant with God is, by that fact, a "people."

Covenant Relationships: Vertical and Horizontal

If we turn back once more to the passage that begins in Exodus, chapter 19, where God enters into a covenant with Israel, we discover a second, related principle: The same covenant that brought Israel into a unique relationship with God also, by that fact, brought them into a unique relationship with one another. The main purpose of the following chapters of Exodus (chapters 10 through 23) is to define the specific, practical ways in which God required them, from then onward, to relate to one another. As members of one covenant people, they had special obligations to each other, different from those which they had to members of other nations who had no covenant relationship either with God or with Israel.

We may state this principle more generally, as follows: Those who have a covenant relationship with God necessarily also have a covenant relationship with each other. The relationships established by a covenant extend in two directions: vertical and horizontal. The covenant that brings us into union vertically with God must of necessity also bring us into union horizontally with all who have entered into the same covenant with God. We have no right to claim the benefits of covenant relationship with God, while at the same time refusing to accept our obligations toward those who share the same covenant with Him. The same covenant that brings individuals into union with God also brings them into collective union with one another. It establishes

> THOSE WHO HAVE A COVENANT RELATIONSHIP WITH GOD NECESSARILY ALSO HAVE A COVENANT RELATIONSHIP WITH EACH OTHER.

them collectively as a *"people"* who are set apart from all other collective units of humanity.

These principles concerning covenant established in the Old Testament are carried over, unchanged, into the New Testament. When Jesus celebrated the Last Supper with His disciples and shared with them the bread and the wine, He brought them into a covenant relationship with Himself by that act. After He had handed them the cup and told them all to drink of it, He said, *"This is My blood of the covenant"* (Matthew 26:28). They didn't merely share the cup of the covenant with Him; they also shared it with each other. The solemn act that brought each of them into covenant with Jesus, at the same time brought them all into covenant with one another. From then on, their covenant relationship was not merely vertical, to Jesus; it was also horizontal, to each other.

This is borne out in 1 Corinthians, where Paul explained the significance of the Lord's Supper. He emphasized this horizontal relationship between all who partake of the one loaf and the one cup:

> *Is not the cup of blessing which we bless*
> *a sharing in the blood of Christ? Is not*
> *the bread which we break a sharing in*

the body of Christ? Since there is one bread, we who are many are one body; for we all partake of the one bread.

(1 Corinthians 10:16–17)

Peter also declared that the new covenant in Christ has the same effect as God's previous covenant with Israel: It establishes all who enter into it as a collective *"people"*:

But you are a chosen race, a royal priesthood, a holy nation, a people for God's own possession, that you may proclaim the excellencies of Him who has called you out of darkness into His marvelous light [Peter was quoting the very words spoken by God to Israel in Exodus 19:5–6]; *for you once were not a people, but now you are the people of God; you had not received mercy, but now you have received mercy.* (1 Peter 2:9–10)

In light of this, we should be much more circumspect than most of us are about how and with whom we take communion. By this, I am not advocating a closed communion table. I believe that every Christian has a right to the table of the Lord. However, we must be very careful not to eat and drink ourselves into condemnation.

Therefore whoever eats the bread or drinks the cup of the Lord in an unworthy manner, shall be guilty of the body and the blood of the Lord. But let a man examine himself, and so let him eat of the bread and drink of the cup. For he who eats and drinks, eats and drinks judgment to himself, if he does not judge the body rightly.

(1 Corinthians 11:27–29)

We eat and drink condemnation because we do not discern the Lord's body. This means that we don't discern the sacrifice that Jesus made for us. But it also means that we don't discern the other members of the body of Christ. If we eat and drink out of wrong attitudes and wrong relationships, we eat and drink condemnation, not blessing. Paul went so far as to tell the Corinthian church, *"For this reason many among you are weak and sick, and a number sleep"* (v. 30). It is very serious to be out of covenant with one another, and out of union.

We have already seen in two cases that the end purpose of covenant is union. The purpose of the marriage covenant is to bring a man and a woman into union with each other. The purpose of the covenant between God and the individual believer is to bring the believer into union with God. This principle applies with equal force to the third case—the covenant between believers. Its purpose is to bring all believers into union with each other.

After Jesus had shared the bread and wine of the new covenant with His disciples, He went on to share with them the intimate discourse recorded in John, chapters 14 through 16. This teaching came to its climax with His high-priestly prayer for them in John, chapter 17. This prayer, in turn, culminates with His plea to the Father that all who believe in Him *"may be one, just as We are one"* (v. 22).

THE END PURPOSE OF COVENANT IS UNION.

In this context, we understand that this plea constitutes the outworking of the covenant that He had established with them earlier that evening. The end purpose of the covenant is union of the same nature and quality as that which exists between the Father and the Son. Until we, as believers, have come into this unity, we have not fulfilled our covenant obligations— either to Christ or to one another.

We have already pointed out that when God made His covenant with Israel at Mount Sinai, He immediately explained to the Israelites the obligations that the covenant would impose upon them in their relationships and dealings with one another. These obligations are set out, in specific and practical terms, in Exodus, chapters 20 through 23.

In a corresponding way, the New Testament sets forth, for all who enter into the new covenant in Christ, the ways in which they are obligated, by their covenant commitment, to relate to one another. It is outside the scope of this book to examine in detail all the mutual obligations of believers toward each other. However, we may form a general picture of these obligations by picking out phrases such as *"each other"* or *"one another"* wherever they occur in the New Testament and listing the various mutual obligations that are thereby indicated.

All who have entered into the new covenant in Christ are required to behave in the following ways toward one another:

- Wash one another's feet (John 13:14)
- Love one another (John 13:34, for example)
- Build up one another (Romans 14:19)

- Accept one another (Romans 15:7)
- Admonish one another (Romans 15:14, for example)
- Greet one another (Romans 16:16, for example)
- Serve one another (Galatians 5:13)
- Bear one another's burdens (Galatians 6:2)
- Show forbearance to one another (Ephesians 4:2)
- Forgive one another (Ephesians 4:32, for example)
- Be subject to one another (Ephesians 5:21)
- Teach one another (Colossians 3:16)
- Comfort one another (1 Thessalonians 4:18)
- Encourage one another (Hebrews 3:13)
- Stimulate one another to love and good deeds (Hebrews 10:24)
- Confess sins to one another (James 5:16)
- Pray for one another (James 5:16)
- Be hospitable to one another (1 Peter 4:9)
- Be clothed with humility toward one another (1 Peter 5:5)

Only insofar as we, as believers, discharge these mutual responsibilities toward one another are we fulfilling the terms of the new covenant.

Although the obligations of the new covenant are stated somewhat differently from those of the covenant made at Mount Sinai, the basic principle is, again, the same: Those who enter into a covenant with God are, by that very act, necessarily brought into covenant with one another. The obligations of these covenants extend in two directions: vertically, between the covenant people and God; horizontally, between the members of the covenant people.

Only Death Validates the Covenant

Another principle that applies universally to these covenants is that a covenant is valid only on the basis of the sacrifice. This general principle is stated, as we saw in chapter 2, in Hebrews:

> *For where a covenant is, there must of necessity be the death of the one who made it. For a covenant is valid only when men are dead, for it is never in force while the one who made it lives.*
>
> (Hebrews 9:16–17)

In the next three verses, the writer of Hebrews applied this principle specifically to the covenant between God and Israel, which was mediated by Moses at Mount Sinai:

Therefore even the first covenant was not inaugurated without blood. For when every commandment had been spoken by Moses to all the people according to the Law, he took the blood of the calves and the goats, with water and scarlet wool and hyssop, and sprinkled both the book itself and all the people, saying, "This is the blood of the covenant which God commanded you." (Hebrews 9:18–20)

In each case, the death of the sacrifice represented the death of those who entered by it into the covenant. However, there was an essential difference. The animals sacrificed by Moses merely reminded Israel of the principle that covenant was valid only through death, and prefigured a different kind of sacrifice that had not yet been offered.

On the other hand, the death of Jesus on the cross was substitutionary. He died as the personal representative of all who were to enter into the covenant with God through Him. Jesus identified Himself with each in death, so that each in turn might identify himself with Jesus. As this two-way identification is worked out through the ongoing commitment of each believer, the death of Jesus becomes, effectively and experientially, the death of the believer. This principle was clearly stated by Paul in 2 Corinthians:

> *For the love of Christ controls us, having concluded this, that one died for all, therefore all died; and He died for all, that they who live should no longer live for themselves, but for Him who died and rose again on their behalf.*
>
> (2 Corinthians 5:14–15)

Paul's conclusion is both clear and logical. It is summed up in the words *"therefore all died."* If we accept Christ's death as our death, then we must *"consider* [our]*selves to be dead"* (Romans 6:11). Therefore, we are no longer free to live for ourselves. This, too, has a two-way application: vertically, toward the Lord, and horizontally, toward the Lord's people. When the Lord and Abram entered into covenant with each other, each voluntarily abrogated the right to live only for himself. Each, by the "cutting" of the covenant, said to the other, in effect, "That is my death. As I enter into this covenant, I enter by death. Now that I am in covenant, I have no more right to live."

Marriage Covenant

The same relationship that was established that memorable night, person-to-person, between the Lord and Abram is reestablished among all who, through the death of Jesus, are brought into covenant with each other. Each of us reaffirms the mutual covenant of which the Lord and Abram are the prototype, the original pattern. Each says to the other, "That is my death. As I enter into this covenant, I enter by death. Now that I am in covenant, I have no more right to live."

In 1 John, the apostle specifically applied the outworking of the death that alone makes our covenant valid to our relationship with our fellow believers:

> *We know love by this, that He laid down His life for us; and we ought to lay down our lives for the brethren. But whoever has the world's goods, and beholds his brother in need and closes his heart against him, how does the love of God abide in him?* (1 John 3:16–17)

The phrase *"we ought to"* expresses an obligation—one that we cannot evade if we claim to be partakers of the same covenant. When John spoke about laying down our lives, he was not speaking solely—or even primarily—about undergoing physical death. He made this quite clear, because, in the next verse, he applied it to making our worldly goods available to our fellow believers. If we are not willing to do this where there is a legitimate need, then we are not willing to *"lay down our lives."* Laying down our lives means being ready to share with our covenant brothers and sisters both what we are and what we have. If we are not willing to do this, our covenant commitment is not genuine.

The New Lifestyle—*Koinonia*

In the Greek vocabulary of the New Testament, one very important word describes the distinctive lifestyle into which we are initiated through the new covenant. It is *koinonia*. The noun *koinonia* is derived from the adjective *koinos* (common). Literally and basically, *koinonia* is "having in common." Insofar as two or more persons have things in common, they have *koinonia*. If there are any areas where they do not have things in common, in those areas they do not have *koinonia*. It was said of the early church in Jerusalem, *"All things were common property to them"* (Acts 4:32). That was *koinonia*.

In the majority of English translations of the New Testament, *koinonia* is translated *"fellowship."* However, in some versions it is not translated by a single English word, but by a phrase, such as "to be in union with" or "to share in common life." Because there is no one English word that fully expresses its meanings, in this chapter we will continue to use the word in its Greek form, *koinonia*.

Koinonia is the outworking of true unity. The perfect example of *koinonia* is the relationship between God the Father and God the Son. In John 10:30, Jesus said, *"I and the Father are one."* This unity between the Father and the Son is the basis of their *koinonia*. Jesus described its outworking in John 16:14–15, where He said of the Holy Spirit, *"He shall take of Mine, and shall disclose it to you."* But then He immediately explained, *"All things that the Father has are Mine."* In other words, Jesus said, "All that is Mine I have, not in my own right, but on the basis of My unity with the Father."

In John 17:10, Jesus stated the same again in His prayer to the Father: *"All things that are Mine are Thine, and Thine are Mine."* This is perfect *koinonia*—the having of all things in common.

In this sense, the gospel is an invitation from the Father and the Son to all members of the human race to share with them the perfect *koinonia* that they share with each other. In 1 Corinthians 1:9, Paul said, *"God is faithful, through whom you were called into fellowship [koinonia] with His Son, Jesus Christ our Lord."* It is important to distinguish between "means" and "ends." So many forms of religious activity are "means" rather than "ends." They are not valuable in themselves, but only insofar as they enable us to achieve "ends," which alone are valuable in themselves. *Koinonia*, however, is not merely a "means"—it is an end. It is, in fact, the supreme end of all worthwhile religious activity.

COVENANT IS THE DOOR TO UNITY.

John likewise declared that the end purpose of the gospel is to bring all who respond to its message into the same eternal *koinonia* that the Father and the Son enjoy between themselves:

What we have seen and heard we proclaim to you also, that you also may

145

*have fellowship [koinonia] with us; and
indeed our fellowship [koinonia] is with
the Father, and with His Son Jesus
Christ. And these things we write, so
that our joy may be made complete.*

(1 John 1:3–4)

"What we have seen and heard" is the eye-
witness testimony of Christ's apostles, preserved
for us in the pages of the New Testament. These
verses, therefore, disclose the central purpose
for which God caused the gospel record to be
preserved and transmitted. It is that all who believe and obey may have opportunity to share in
the perfect, eternal *koinonia*, which is the lifestyle of heaven.

The Price of *Koinonia*

However, *koinonia* is not cheap. There is a
price to pay. The cost is set by two unvarying
requirements. The first is commitment; the second is a way of life that is called *"walk*[ing] *in
the light"* (1 John 1:7).

Covenant, as we have seen, is the door to
unity. Only those who are willing to make the
total, unreserved commitment of a covenant
can ever come into true unity with each other.
This applies alike in the relationship between

146

husband and wife, between the believer and God, and between believers in fellowship together.

Thereafter, this commitment is worked out through walking in the light. John said, *"But if we walk in the light as He Himself is in the light, we have fellowship [koinonia] with one another"* (1 John 1:7). Walking in the light is the only way to experience *koinonia*. Wherever Scripture speaks of *koinonia*, it acknowledges only one standard—that of God Himself. It is expressed here by the phrase, *"as He Himself is in the light."* God is willing to lift humanity up to His own level of *koinonia*, but He is not willing to lower the standard of *koinonia* to that of unredeemed humanity—or even of backslidden Christendom.

> WHEREVER DISHONESTY OR INSINCERITY OR SELFISH RESERVATIONS CREEP IN, THE LIGHT BEGINS TO DIM.

At the same time, the phrase *"in the light"* sets boundaries to what may be shared in *koinonia*. Anything that contravenes divine law in the realm of morals or ethics is not *"in the light."* On the contrary, it is darkness. An obvious example is in the area of sexual relationship. It is in accordance with divine law for a husband and wife to have sexual relationship with each other. This is fully *"in the light."* But for either of them to have sexual relationship with any other person is contrary to divine law. It is no longer *"in the light."*

Subject to this reservation, however, walking in the light is a relationship of total, continuing honesty and openness between all who are in *koinonia*. Nothing may be hidden or misrepresented or held back. The essence of the relationship is the same whether it is between a husband and wife or among a group of believers who are committed to each other. We may sum it up in the words that we used in chapter 3 to describe the husband/wife relationship: a total, unreserved opening up of each personality to the others.

Thus, the limits of *koinonia* are governed by two factors: divine law and absolute honesty. Divine law sets the boundaries; whatever contravenes divine law is no longer *koinonia*. It is darkness, not light. But within those boundaries, the light must be full and unrestricted. Wherever dishonesty or insincerity or selfish reservations creep in, the light begins to dim. *Koinonia* is no longer on the divine level.

What shall we say of Christians who seek fellowship one with another, but are not willing to meet these requirements? Logically, we must say the same as we would of a man and a woman who seek a sexual relationship but are not willing to meet the requirements for marriage. The result that they achieve is not *koinonia,* but

> WALKING IN THE LIGHT IS A RELATIONSHIP OF TOTAL, CONTINUING HONESTY AND OPENNESS BETWEEN ALL WHO ARE IN *KOINONIA.*

fornication. This is equally true whether it is on the physical plane between a man and a woman, or on the spiritual plane between Christians who seek a permanent relationship with each other. Those who refuse God's requirements are, by His standards, guilty of fornication. That there is such a thing as spiritual fornication is attested by the Old Testament, whose prophets charged Israel with this very sin repeatedly.

The results of such wrong, uncommitted relationships between Christians in a group are very similar to those that develop between a man and a woman in a wrong sexual relationship. The results are hurts, bitterness, strife, broken relationships, unfulfilled promises, and unsatisfied yearnings. When we judge by results, we are compelled to acknowledge that, in many sections of professing Christendom today, there is little evidence of true *koinonia,* but abundant evidence of wholesale spiritual fornication.

Our purpose in this chapter has been to set forth as clearly as possible the scriptural remedy for this tragic situation. It lies in a return to God's requirements: covenant commitment that is walked out *"in the light."*

SEVEN

The Point of Decision

CHAPTER 7

The Point of Decision

In the preceding chapters, we have dealt with three of the most important relationships in life. In order of priority, they are: our personal relationship with God, our marital relationship (if we are married), and our relationship with God's believing people. In each of these areas, we have seen the type of relationship that God has made available to those who will believe and obey Him.

Perhaps you have come to realize that you have been living on too low a level in one or more of these areas. You are ready to move up to a new level, but you are not sure how to do it. Let me remind you, therefore, that in every case you will find that there is one simple but essential requirement. It is expressed by a word that we have used many times in this book: *commitment.*

Marriage Covenant

Commitment to God

Let me speak first about the area of your personal relationship with God. You may be a churchgoer, or at least have a church background. You may be familiar with the accepted phrases used by religious people. You may actually have experienced moments of uplift or inspiration when you knew that God was real.

Alternatively, you may be a person with no church background. Although you are not an adherent of any definite religion, there is a hunger in your heart that you long to satisfy.

Or again, you may not belong to either of these categories. You may have come to this moment by some unique route of your own. That really is not the issue just now. What matters is that you have come to a point where you long for an intimate, personal relationship with God— something so deep and real that you will never again need to question it. You are ready, therefore, to make a sincere, wholehearted commitment of yourself to God through Jesus Christ.

The natural way for you to make your commitment is by prayer. In this way, you give expression to what is in your heart; in the process of verbalizing it, you give it content. You make your commitment *specific*. A prayer of this kind is like crossing a bridge. It takes you over into new territory. From this moment on, you will not be relying on something vague and undefined in the shadowy realm of your mind. After praying, you will know *what* you are committed to. You will also know *when* and *where* you made your commitment. Your ongoing relationship with God will henceforth have a definite starting point—something fixed in a time-space world—a point of decision.

My counsel is that you put the book down right now and pray! If you feel able to pray in your own words, then do so. But if you find that difficult, here is a prepared prayer for you to use:

God,

You have put a desire in my heart to know You in a real and personal way. Even if I do not fully understand everything, I believe what the Bible says about Jesus Christ: that He took my sins upon Himself, died in my place, and rose again from the dead. In His name, I ask You now to forgive all my sins and to receive me as Your child. Sincerely, and with my whole heart, I commit myself to You—all I am and all I have. Take me as I am, and make me what You want me to be. In faith, I believe You do hear this prayer, and You do receive me. I thank You.

> In Jesus' name, amen.

Once you have prayed your prayer of commitment, do not begin to reason or speculate. In simple faith, take God at His word. He has promised to receive you if you come to Him through Jesus Christ. Thank Him, therefore, that He has done what He promised. Keep on thanking Him! The more you thank Him, the more your faith will grow.

From now on, make it your main aim to cultivate your new relationship with God. This will give you a simple standard by which to evaluate the various influences and activities in your life: Do they strengthen your relationship with God, or do they weaken it? Make more and more room for the things that strengthen it, and less and less for those that weaken it. Specifically, there are two ways to strengthen the relationship that are particularly important.

First, make your commitment known to those around you. You will not need to be aggressive or to put on religious airs. But as opportunities come in the normal course of daily life, make it known in a quiet but firm way that Jesus is now in full control of your life.

Second, set aside a period of each day for God. Spend part of this period reading your Bible and part of it praying—that is, talking to God in a sincere and natural way. In this way, you will maintain an ongoing two-way communication with God. As you read your Bible, God will speak to you. As you pray, you will speak to God.

> REMEMBER, COMMITMENT IS A TWO-WAY STREET. NOT ONLY ARE YOU COMMITTED TO GOD; HE IS ALSO COMMITTED TO YOU.

You will not be expected to achieve instant sainthood! If you fail from time to time, do not become discouraged. Simply acknowledge your failures to God and ask Him to forgive you. *"If we confess our sins, He is faithful and righteous to forgive us our sins and to cleanse us from all unrighteousness"* (1 John 1:9). If other people are affected by your failures, you may need to ask them also for forgiveness. But do not give up! Remember, commitment is a two-way street. Not only are you committed to God; He is also committed to you. And He is omnipotent!

Commitment to Your Mate

The second area that we have dealt with—in order of priority—is your relationship to your mate, husband or wife as the case may be. (Of course, if you are not married at present and not expecting to marry, this section does not directly concern you.)

You may already have been a committed believer before you read this book. Or again, you may just have prayed a prayer of commitment after reading the previous section. But either way, you are now face to face with the fact that your marriage is not what it ought to be. Perhaps you have realized for the first time what it could be. You have come to understand that, for committed believers, marriage is *"a cord of three strands"* (Ecclesiastes 4:12)—a covenant between you, your mate, and God. But it will take your personal commitment to make the covenant effective, and thus to release into your marriage the vital element that has hitherto been missing: the all-sufficient, supernatural grace of God.

Ideally, you and your mate should both make the commitment at the same time, to God and to each other. However, it sometimes happens that one party is ready before the other. So if you are ready, but your mate is not, make your commitment now and trust God to bring your mate to the same point that you have already reached— the point of decision. Then, when that happens, you can renew your commitment together.

If you feel able to pray in your own words, do so. Otherwise, here is a prepared prayer that you may use to make a covenant commitment to your mate before God:

Father God,

I come to You in the name of Jesus, my Savior and Lord. I thank You that You redeemed me through the blood of Jesus and that I belong to You. I thank You for my marriage. I thank You for my mate. At this moment, I want to commit myself to You, to my marriage, and to my mate. I am ready, Lord, to lay down my life and live it out through my mate, seeking my mate's good before my own, rejoicing in my mate's blessing and my mate's success, counting it as mine, living now in the life of my mate. Father God, accept

this commitment in the name of Jesus.
Set the seal of Your Holy Spirit upon it.
Bless our marriage and our home in a
new way from this day forward.

In Jesus' name, amen.

In the previous section, Commitment to God,
we recommended certain simple steps to make
that commitment effective. For the most part,
the same prin-
ciples apply to the
commitment you
have now made to
your mate and to
your marriage.

> "WORK AT IT!
> BE PATIENT WITH
> ONE ANOTHER.

First of all, make sure that your priorities
are in the right order. Quite probably, this may
necessitate some adjustments. After your personal relationship to God, the next most important area of your life is your marriage and your
home. Evaluate your various activities accord-
ingly. Make more and more room for those that
strengthen your marriage and your home, and
less and less for those that have the opposite effect.

In connection with your personal relationship with God, we pointed out the need to set

aside time to maintain two-way communications with Him. The same applies to your relationship with your mate. Open, continuing communication between the two of you is vital. It will take time—more time, probably, than you have been giving to it. Remember, the way you allocate your time is the surest indication of your real priorities. You may say that your marriage is important to you, but if you allow disproportionate amounts of time to other activities, you are really giving them priority over your marriage.

Someone coined the saying, "The family that prays together stays together." There is a great deal of truth in it. For thirty years, Lydia and I prayed and read the Bible together almost every day—usually twice a day. Often, God spoke to us in a very intimate way in these times of communication with Him and with each other. They were one of the principle factors in the success of our marriage.

Sometimes, I have observed that husbands and wives find it difficult to pray out loud in each other's presence. It seems hard to break through the "sound barrier." But work at it! Be patient with one another. The benefits will far outweigh any initial embarrassment or sense of strangeness. When you and your mate can freely talk to God in each other's presence, it is sure proof that God has really become a member of your family—which is what He longs to be.

One last word on this subject: Never again rely solely on your own effort and ability to make your marriage a success. No marriage can ever be what God intends it to be apart from His supernatural grace. The commitment you have now made to your mate and your marriage has made that grace available to you in a measure that you have never known before. Avail yourself of it freely! God has told us, *"My grace is sufficient for you, for power is perfected in weakness"* (2 Corinthians 12:9). God's grace and power will see you through every difficulty that arises. If you feel perplexed, discouraged, or inadequate, trust God for an extra measure of grace and power, right then and there. Expect to see Him work—in ways, perhaps, you could never have imagined. Expect to see Him change whatever needs to be changed—you, your mate, the whole situation. He will not fail you.

Commitment to God's People

The third area of relationship that we have dealt with in this book is that which we have called *koinonia*—the sharing of your life with God's people. For true spiritual fulfillment you need this kind of relationship. Without it, you can never be all that God intends you to be. This is equally true for single people and for married couples. All of us need to be part of something larger than ourselves.

In 1 Corinthians 12:13–27, Paul compared individual believers to the various parts that make up a single body. He explained that no part can function effectively on its

> NO MARRIAGE CAN EVER BE WHAT GOD INTENDS IT TO BE APART FROM HIS SUPERNATURAL GRACE.

own. Each needs the others. *"And the eye cannot say to the hand, 'I have no need of you'; or again the head to the feet, 'I have no need of you'"* (verse 21). As individual believers, we can achieve true fulfillment and wholeness only by entering into a committed relationship with other believers in such a way that we can, together with them, function as a single body.

A relationship of this kind is not optional. It is essential for our own spiritual well-being.

Let us look once more at a verse that has been quoted earlier: *"But if we walk in the light as He Himself is in the light, we have fellowship [koinonia] with one another, and the blood of Jesus His Son cleanses us from all sin"* (1 John 1:7).

The introductory *"if"* confronts us with two related facts of spiritual experience. First, the primary evidence that we are walking in the light is that we have *koinonia* with one another. If we do not have this relationship of *koinonia* with other believers, it is normally evidence that we are not walking fully in the light. Second, if we are not in the light of *koinonia*, we no longer experience the continuous cleansing of the blood of Jesus, which alone can keep us pure and free from sin.

Our responsibility for regular fellowship with a group of committed believers is stated in Hebrews:

> *And let us consider how to stimulate one another to love and good deeds, not forsaking our own assembling together, as is the habit of some, but encouraging one another; and all the more, as you see the day drawing near.* (Hebrews 10:24–25)

Here again, we have two related truths: First, we are responsible to stimulate and encourage one another; second, we can do this only if we do not forsake *"our own assembling."* This last phrase obviously takes it for granted that all of us will be related to a group that we can properly call "our own assembly."

The essential step that brings us into this kind of relationship is the same that brings us into proper relationship with God or with our mates. It is *commitment*—not just to another individual, however, but to a group of people who are themselves united in mutual commitment. If you have already made the first two commitments dealt with in this chapter—to God and to your mate—you should follow these with this third form of commitment—to a group of fellow believers.

Unfortunately, it is not always easy, in contemporary Christendom, to find a group that is practicing real, mutual commitment on a sound, scriptural basis. However, if you acknowledge to God your need to identify with such a group and then go on to seek Him diligently for His direction, you can be confident that He will show you what to do. Remember that God has promised to reward those who seek Him. (See Hebrews

11:6.) If you are sincere and earnest in seeking Him, you will receive your reward.

As a guideline to recognize the kind of group that will fulfill your need, here are nine questions you should ask before you make any definite commitment:

1. Do they honor and uplift the Lord Jesus Christ?
2. Do they respect the authority of Scripture?
3. Do they make room for the moving of the Holy Spirit?
4. Do they exhibit a warm and friendly attitude?
5. Do they seek to work out their faith in practical, day-to-day living?
6. Do they build interpersonal relationships among themselves that go beyond merely attending services?
7. Do they provide pastoral care that embraces all your legitimate needs?
8. Are they open to fellowship with other Christian groups?
9. Do you feel at ease and at home among them?

If the answer to all or most of these questions is "yes," you are getting warm. Continue to seek God, however, until you receive definite direction from Him. Remember that you will not find "the perfect group." Furthermore, even if you did, you could not join it, because after you did, it would no longer be perfect!

Finally, here is a word of encouragement, but also of warning:

> *God makes a home for the lonely; He leads out the prisoners into prosperity, only the rebellious dwell in a parched land.* (Psalm 68:6)

If you are *"lonely,"* God will place you in a spiritual *"home"*—a family of Christian brothers and sisters united in mutual commitment to one another. If you are a "prisoner" of circumstances or evil forces, God will deliver you and bring you out into freedom. But—and here is the warning—if you are *"rebellious,"* you will continue to *"dwell in a parched land."*

Ultimately, the only barriers that can keep you from finding the kind of *koinonia* you need will be your own inner attitudes of pride, selfishness, or unyielding individualism. Ask God to show you if there are any such barriers in your life and, if they do exist, to break them down.

In Psalm 27:4, David gave utterance to the deepest longing of his soul:

One thing I have asked from the Lord, that I shall seek; that I may dwell in the house of the Lord all the days of my life....

Do these words of David express the deep longing of your soul? If so, why not echo them in a prayer of your own?

Once again, if you feel able to pray in your own words, do that. But if you prefer a prepared prayer, you may use the following:

Lord,

I am lonely and unfulfilled, and I acknowledge it. I long to *"dwell in Your house"*—to be part of a spiritual "family" of committed believers. If there are any barriers in me, I ask You to remove them. Guide me to a group where this longing of mine can be fulfilled, and help me to make the needed commitment to them.

In the name of Jesus, amen.

About the Author,
Derek Prince

About the Author

D erek Prince (1915–2003) was born in Bangalore, India, into a British military family. He was educated as a scholar of classical languages (Greek, Latin, Hebrew, and Aramaic) at Eton College and Cambridge University in England and later at Hebrew University, Israel. As a student, he was a philosopher and self-proclaimed atheist. He held a fellowship in ancient and modern philosophy at King's College, Cambridge.

While in the British Medical Corps during World War II, Prince began to study the Bible as a philosophical work. Converted through a powerful encounter with Jesus Christ, he was baptized in the Holy Spirit a few days later. This life-changing experience altered the whole course of his life, which he thereafter devoted to studying and teaching the Bible as the Word of God.

Discharged from the army in Jerusalem in 1945, he married Lydia Christensen, founder of a children's home there. Upon their marriage, he immediately became father to Lydia's eight adopted daughters—six Jewish, one Palestinian Arab, one English. Together the family saw the rebirth of the state of Israel in 1948. In the late 1950s the Princes adopted another daughter while he was serving as principal of a college in Kenya.

In 1963 the Princes immigrated to the United States and pastored a church in Seattle. Stirred by the tragedy of John F. Kennedy's assassination, he began to teach Americans how to intercede for their nation. In 1973 he became one of the founders of Intercessors for America. His book *Shaping History through Prayer and Fasting* has awakened Christians around the world to their responsibility to pray for their governments. Many consider underground translations of the book as instrumental in the fall of communist regimes in the USSR, East Germany, and Czechoslovakia.

Lydia Prince died in 1975, and Derek married Ruth Baker (a single mother to three adopted children) in 1978. He met his second wife, like his first, while he was serving the Lord in Jerusalem. Ruth died in December 1998 in Jerusalem where they had lived since 1981.

Until a few years before his own death in 2003 at the age of eighty-eight, Prince persisted in the ministry God had called him to as he traveled the world, imparting God's revealed truth, praying for the sick and afflicted, and sharing his prophetic insights into world events in the light of Scripture. He wrote over fifty books, which have been translated in over sixty languages and distributed worldwide. He pioneered teaching on such groundbreaking themes as generational curses, the biblical significance of Israel, and demonology.

Derek Prince Ministries, with its international headquarters in Charlotte, North Carolina, continues to distribute his teachings and to train missionaries, church leaders, and congregations through its worldwide branch offices. His radio program, *Keys to Successful Living* (now known as *Derek Prince Legacy Radio*), began in 1979 and has been translated into over a dozen languages. Estimates are that Derek Prince's clear, nondenominational, nonsectarian teaching of the Bible has reached more than half the globe.

Internationally recognized as a Bible scholar and spiritual patriarch, Derek Prince established a teaching ministry that spanned six continents and more than sixty years. In 2002 he said, "It is my desire—and I believe the Lord's desire—that this ministry continue the work, which God began through me over sixty years ago, until Jesus returns."